To Amy,
love in
Jesus,
Davie'
Phil 4:13

Always too soon
to Quit

Always too soon
to Quit

Nancy Bramlett
with Tula Jeffries

Printed in the United States

Cover designed by Adrienne Renae Rogers
Beach Portrait-Courtesy of Gallery One Portrait Studio-Destin, FL.

Scripture quotations are from THE KING JAMES VERSION of the Bible.

Library of Congress Cataloging-in-Publication Data

Bramlett, Nancy.
    Always too soon to Quit : the Nancy Bramlett story / by Nancy Bramlett with Tula Jeffries.
        p.   cm.
    Includes bibliographical references.

    1. Bramlett, Nancy.
I. Jeffries, Tula, 1921–   II. Title.

Acknowledgements

The writing of this book has been the hardest achievement in my life.

There is no way to express my love and appreciation to Tula Jeffries for writing my story. She wrote John's book *"Taming the Bull,"* and probably knows more about us than anyone. She is a godly and giving woman, and is beautiful on the inside and the out. The Lord truly sent her into our lives to tell our stories of what Jesus can do in impossible situations.

Through tears and laughter, I have opened my heart to each one who reads this story.

I also want to especially thank Joyce Morton, for her many hours of recording so many of my thoughts. She was a blessing and helped make this book a reality.

I also want to acknowledge the many friends (I call them my cheerleaders) that have stood by me and encouraged me with finishing this book.

Last, but not least—my family. I was blessed to be raised with much love and security from my family. This, I'm sure is one of the main reasons I was able to endure my turbulent marriage for those many years. I'm very grateful for my heritage and so very thankful for my family today.

I had many reasons for choosing the title "Always too Soon to Quit." I know through the years in my own life, and many of the women I have counseled, that we can not control the choices of others. We need to always be careful not to judge others actions if we haven't walked in their shoes.

My story was not an easy one to share, but felt in my heart, if it could help one person come to the Lord or to walk closer to Him, I was glad to bare my soul.

I first heard the title for my book from a Godly Bible teacher, Faye Hardy, over 20 years ago. She is a very special friend and someone that every time you are with her you learn more about the Lord Jesus. "Always Too Soon To Quit" spoke to my heart and spirit and I quickly wrote it in the front of my Bible. I never imagined at that time it would be the title of my book, but He who understands us best, always knew.

Foreword

Always too soon to Quit can be a life-changing book. It has certainly been a great blessing to me.

This book will be a great encouragement to those in desperate situations. (Facing an unwanted divorce, discovery of an unfaithful mate, living in an abusive or unloving relationship.)

Every wife will receive helpful information how to give loving support to her man whatever his lifestyle. Those who know the Lord will feel their hearts singing as they read this astounding story of God's matchless love and grace.

This book can also be given as a gift to lovingly share Christ with a friend.

Get ready for a very frank story. Nancy writes with candor that is refreshing and brings stark realism and an inside look into the home and heart of a stellar athlete and his wife, who apart from the grace of God would have seen their home broken beyond repair.

I've known Nancy personally for twenty-five years; and I can testify that she lives what she teaches and teaches what she lives.

Joyce Rogers
Author, Speaker, Wife of Dr. Adrian Rogers, Pastor Emeritus of Bellevue Baptist Church and Founder of Love Worth Finding Ministries

I tug at my mind, trying to free it from the foggy abyss it is locked in. I hear birds chirping outside my bedroom window, and idly wonder at the happy sounds of these tiny, tranquil creatures. Don't they know better than to set themselves up for a fall? If spared by one quirk of fate, don't they know that the next door neighbor's cat, Midnight, is always waiting to pounce?

I feel something pinching my waist and realize I am still wearing the tight pants and shirt of the night before. Blinking in the early morning light, I have trouble focusing. In a rush of sudden nausea, I hear again the voice of a secretary who works in John's office. Grabbing my arm as John and I leave a popular lounge, she says loudly, "Your husband tried to get me to go to an apartment with him this week and I think you need to know it."

I stand frozen to the floor, my mouth open in disbelief, my face burns as I try to swallow the tears that spring to my eyes. Her look of pity tells me she is speaking the truth. Unable to face the startled expressions on the faces nearest us, I stumble toward the door. The guilty alarm on John's face confirms her accusation.

Holding my arm, his face contorted with anger, he says, "Nancy, that's a lie! Can't you see, she's making the whole thing up?" He glares at the woman as if he wants to kill her, but she returns his gaze steadily. By then several people are gathering around to watch, so I rush blindly out the door. Stumbling out to the parking lot, I just want to find our car and leave. John is still holding on to me, still pleading his case.

"Nancy, honey, listen to me! That woman is lying! How could you be stupid enough to fall for that? She's half drunk, for godsakes! Can't you see she's just trying to get me in trouble? Don't be dumb enough to fall for her lies!" By now, we are out of the parking lot and driving down the street.

"She is not lying, and you know it! I'm not as dumb as you think! I want to know what she is talking about. Where is this apartment? How many other women have you taken there with you? I thought our marriage meant something to you," I sob.

"Honey, it does, it means everything to me. I told you, she's just making it up. It never happened, Nancy, I swear!"

"I can't live like this," I scream. "If this is the way its going to be, I can't do it! I don't want to live like this." Hysterical, I open the car door to jump, but John's quickness stops me. He grips my arm, and I see the fear in his face as we pass under a street light. He is begging me to calm down and shut the door. For once, he seems to be in a situation he doesn't know how to handle.

I don't know if I would have jumped. I know I would have regretted it before I hit the pavement, but after a few minutes of John begging me to believe him, he curses at that lying woman, and I close the door and settle into a miserable silence.

John keeps a cautious eye on me but says nothing as I walk stoically into our bedroom and fall across the bed. I turn off the light. For once, he is quiet and subdued.

It is not mentioned again. My life... my future... is going down the sewer, and I'm too scared to talk about it.

~ *Chapter One* ~

An idyllic childhood was probably poor preparation for the harsh realities of a life with John Bramlett. I grew up on Hollywood, near North Parkway and Overton Park in Memphis. The large, attractive homes with their neatly manicured lawns and wide, shaded streets were a far cry from the ramshackle collection of timeworn houses of John's neighborhood. Alabama Street, with its squalid rows of shotgun style houses, some with outhouses perched in the back, was miles away and a world apart from Hollywood Street. An affront to John's pride, his background seemed to inflate the sizable chip he carried on his shoulder every place he went.

When I met John for the first time, I already knew something of his reputation. He was a stellar athlete, but even as only a high school junior, he was known as being mean and tough; the local "bad boy."

One night, driving around with a group of girls from my school, Central High, we ran into several boys from Humes High at our favorite drive-in. One of the girls with us knew the boys from the rival school, so she began introductions all around. One of the boys already had my attention; he was the best looking boy I'd ever seen, and suddenly I heard Rita saying, "Nancy, this is John Bramlett."

In that first moment of eye contact, my heart began racing. I suddenly felt ten years old and speechless, but after his shy, "Hi, nice to meet you," he was very quiet, not at all what I expected. When I sneaked an occasional look at him, his eyes were on mine and I could see that he was as nervous and flustered as I felt. After we all left the drive-in, I couldn't stop thinking about him. There was something behind that shy smile that triggered strong feelings in me and that last quick look from him told me he felt something, too.

All the way home, I was scheming up ways to run into him again. I tried to calm down by telling myself that he probably had all the girls over at Humes High chasing him.

A few days later, he called me. I recognized his voice the instant I heard it, but he identified himself as "a friend of John Bramlett's."

"I was with John at the drive-in that night we met," he said.

"Oh really? What's your name?"

"That doesn't matter... I'm just calling to see what you thought of John."

My heart was thumping so fast I could hardly speak. I knew the voice on the phone belonged to John, but I played along to see what he would say. I was hoping he would ask me out.

"So, what did you think about him?"

"Oh, I thought he was real nice," I answered, trying to keep from laughing. "Would you go out with him if he asked you?"

"Yeah, I think I would. Sure."

"You would! Man, that's great! I mean, I'll tell John you said, Yes."

My heart went out to him as I realized that he was so afraid of being rejected that he had to hide behind a lie. It was no longer funny. I just wanted to put him at ease, so I made conversation about school and our mutual friends. After a few minutes, he said, "Well, like I said, I'll tell John you said you would date him. He will probably call you soon."

A few days after that scintillating conversation, John showed up on my doorstep. He was there to invite me to go to church with him on Sunday night. Not a word about his "friend's" call! I didn't mention it either. I guess he thought a date for church was safe enough to get past my parents, and it was. The next three Sunday nights, we went to John's family's church.

I was thrilled to be seen with him; he was different from anyone I had ever met, and I was flattered by his attention. I was so infatuated that I would have spent every minute with him. I hated that he lived so far away. He didn't have a car, so he had to ride the bus or hitchhike to get to my house. He was careful to cultivate a favorable impression on my folks, always very courteous. Not long after we began dating, my parents were doing some painting and wallpapering in the house, and John came over to help.

Dad immediately started a conversation. "So you play football for Humes, do you?"

"Yes sir, I do."

"What position do you play?"

"Linebacker, sir."

"Think you can beat Central this year?"

I listened for John's reply. "I don't know, sir, but we're sure gonna try. Maybe this will be our year, you never can tell!" That was the most I had heard John say at any one time. *He might be shy with me,* I thought, *but he doesn't have any trouble talking about football.*

My dad, Warren Andrews, was president of Innkeepers, a division of Holiday Inns. He met my mother, Adelaide, (whom everyone called Ad) in Draughon's Business College, where both were preparing for a career in the business world. They married in April, prior to the bombing of Pearl Harbor and I was born on Good Friday in April of 1942. Eight years later, my little sister, Janet, arrived on the scene. My mom never used her business training outside the home, but the discipline of its application seeped into her management of our lifestyle.

Family was a top priority to the Andrews clan. My paternal grandmother, Mama Lotta, lived nearby, and I kept the path hot to her house during my early years. When anything upset me, she'd hug me to her and say "everything was going to be all right." She was the most positive person I ever knew.

I'm sure all of those Saturday night dinners at Mama Lotta and Big Daddy's house with aunts, uncles and cousins, influenced my reluctance to give up on any difficult family situation. The moral climate of that time was to stick together and work things out. I still remember the aroma of steaks and chicken cooking on the grill as we all shared family news and events of the week. I often think back to the innocence and carefree atmosphere of those years.

John's lifestyle was lived out at the other end of the spectrum. We knew his background. None of that mattered; my family accepted people on principle rather than on their prestige. We knew how disciplined John was as an athlete, and he worked hard at finding jobs to earn spending money in his spare time. I knew he didn't have money for all the extras many young people enjoy—I didn't care; I just wanted to be with him.

I knew the magnetism I felt was mutual. He spent every minute he could at my house. We dreamed and schemed up ways to be together, and talked constantly of when we could be together forever.

~ *Chapter Two* ~

I've often wondered if my parents were fully aware of the intensity of my feelings for John. Perhaps they guessed, and cautiously avoided making too much of the relationship for fear they would only complicate matters. I'm certain they would have preferred that John accept a football scholarship far from Memphis, and allow us to drift apart after he graduated, I still had a year of high school to go.

His Junior-Senior Prom at Humes was coming up and I was ecstatic in my first floor-length formal gown. On the afternoon of the prom, I was waltzing around the room to the strains of our favorite song when the doorbell rang, and a florist's box was delivered for me. When I opened it, my heart sank. All week long my friends and I had talked of nothing else, and we were certain I would have an orchid to wear. The carnation corsage looked so ordinary, I burst into tears. When he called to see if it had been delivered, I didn't hide my disappointment.

"This is such a special night," I pouted; "I thought you would give me orchids. Every girl but me will have orchids."

"I didn't know," he said; "Honey, you know how special you are to me! If I'd known what you wanted, you'd have the biggest orchid there. I'd do anything to make you happy don't you know that?"

"Well, I'll wear it. If anyone says anything about it, I'll just say you didn't know what to get."

"I didn't, honest! I'm sorry. I'll be there at seven to pick you up."

"Okay," I conceded grudgingly. I found it impossible to stay angry with him. When he came to get me, he had a big white orchid corsage in his hand. I learned years later how he paid for those two corsages. In his neighborhood, when people were desperate for money, they went to the hospital nearby and sold a pint of their blood. He had already sold a pint to buy the carnations, and when he realized my disappointment, he had gone to another hospital, and sold another pint. In all the time we dated, I think every gift he bought me was purchased with his blood.

It was a perfect evening. We danced almost every dance together, refusing to share our happiness in each other with anyone. John was on top of the world. He had been named to All-Memphis, All-State, and All West Tennessee football teams. He was chosen to play in the High School All-American game at Baton Rouge, Louisiana.

I was proud of John's accomplishments, but as his graduation came nearer, I was having to face the fact that the honors he had received could take him somewhere far away. I knew Memphis State (since renamed the University of Memphis) had offered him a football scholarship but so had schools in Tennessee and Kentucky. In spite of all his assurances that there would never be anyone for him but me, I was certain that he would forget me if he went away without me.

I could see the tension in John mounting as the time approached for him to make a decision, and I was desperate for him to choose the local university. One night as we held each other closely, I think we both realized that the intensity of our emotion was almost at the breaking point. It was becoming harder and harder to keep our feelings in check, like trying to stop a smoldering fire from erupting.

John abruptly pulled away from me. "Nancy, I can't stand much more of this! Maybe we ought to get married right now!"

We had talked about marriage before, but always as an event out there in the future. Suddenly, it made perfect sense; the answer to all of our problems.

"We could run away, Nancy... get married in Texarkana! You don't need the consent of your parents down there. You don't even have a waiting period. We can slip off and be married before anyone even knows we're gone. Then wherever I go to college, you can go with me."

"Oh, John," I cried out, throwing myself back into his arms. "That would be wonderful! Let's do it. Let's elope!"

From that moment on, when we were together that's all we talked about. Not once did it occur to us to discuss the serious consequences of what we were planning. It was going to be such fun!

A few weeks later, John accepted Memphis State's offer to play football for them, and we celebrated by secretly setting our wedding date. We were so happy and excited I can't believe someone wouldn't have noticed the change in us. They probably saw our exuberance as relief to have John's big decision behind him. Friends and family alike were glad he had decided to play where he grew up.

I saw myself as a big part of John's dream to make a name for himself through sports. I can see now that my youthful approach to everything was self-serving and headstrong. I made decisions based on very selfish reasoning. I didn't worry about how hurt my parents would be if I didn't finish that last year of high school. I wasn't concerned about how we would support ourselves. I thought only of what I wanted, and what I wanted was John Bramlett. True, he was a little rough around the edges, but I would change all that after we were married.

The day we chose to get married disavows any superstitious thought we might have had; we were married on the thirteenth day of July. Our carefully laid plan for getting away without arousing suspicion was as far as our thinking went; our way of solving problems was to worry about them when they slapped us in the face, not before.

We left town on a Sunday evening after church with John's brother, Burt. He drove us across state and county lines to Texarkana, Texas, over three hundred miles away. The next morning, we went looking for the sources we needed: a place to get a blood test, someone to issue a marriage license, and a justice of the peace to perform the ceremony. Everything went smoothly. Oddly even found a church pastor for us, which somehow made it seem less ill-advised.

Standing there before the minister repeating the marriage vows, the fleeting vision of myself in a beautiful, white wedding gown flashed before me but quickly vanished at the sound of John's voice, clearly stating, "I do." After hours of riding in the car, the orange suit and floral print shoes I had worn to church in Memphis the previous night, suddenly made me feel more like a frightened child than a sophisticated bride on a grand adventure.

When the ceremony was over and we were on our way home, the impact of what we had done settled in on me. I had cleared the way to be out late on Sunday evening, but by now it would be apparent to my parents that we were gone. Together. There was only one thing to do: just come clean and explain our feelings. Cry to make them see that we could make it work, that we *would* make it work. And beg for their forgiveness.

I think they had it all figured out before we got there. All the acrimony we deserved and expected never happened. They swallowed their disappointment, and accepted John graciously. His relief was obvious. Maybe that was why, even at his worst, he has always had the greatest respect for their feelings. I was grateful for the civility he showed them, but learned right away that it didn't necessarily extend to me.

Right from the beginning, I should have known that sports would be the center of our lives. We spent our honeymoon in Baton Rouge where John played in the High School All-American football game. The game was important to John because he had set his heart on one day playing professional ball, and he knew there would be coaches and scouts from all over the country there to watch. And it was clear to me that for the next four years, we would walk, talk, eat and sleep *sports*.

It was a big day for John. His hitting got all the scouts attention, and coaches from Kentucky, Louisiana and Florida were talking with him about his commitment to Memphis State. But we were satisfied with his decision, and have never regretted it.

~ *Chapter Three* ~

After John's scholarship agreement was finalized with Memphis State, we moved into Vets Village. The Village was a group of old army barracks near campus where the married students lived. Each barrack was divided into four apartments. I could hardly wait to get in and start transforming this barren place into a cozy little home. I was certain that with my mother's talent for decorating, 13-A would be the envy of all our friends. I was excitedly reading the home improvement magazines, picking up tips on creating the perfect backdrop for our romantic love nest.

Although my thinking might have been unrealistic, the results were not. With my mother's help and the furniture and accessories she and friends brought over to the apartment, we soon had its drabness converted into an attractive home. I was thrilled when our place was the inspiration for a local newspaper feature on what could be done at little cost in Vets Village with imagination, wallpaper and paint.

John walked, talked, slept and ate sports. If there was a game, any game, any time, anywhere, he became involved. My game was "stretching the dollar." I had once looked for bargains on make-up, perfume, and pretty clothes; now my interest was on the best buys in the supermarket. I kept the scissors ready to clip coupons for savings. Whatever was on special was what we were having for dinner.

Coach Billy Murphy helped me get a job as ROTC secretary to Colonel Gabe Hawkins, Air Science professor in the college. It didn't pay much but added to the fifty-five dollar a month allowance that John got as a married athlete on scholarship, we could manage.

I had never worked at anything outside the home; not even as a Christmas holiday salesgirl. Here I was in this poor man's office trying to balance figures and type reports as if I knew what I was doing when I could barely type. Colonel Hawkins had to be a man of unbelievable patience. I worked for him three years.

No one in Vets Village had any money beyond what was needed for necessities, so we were all constantly looking for ways to get together and have fun for free. The wives shared recipes and ideas for stretching the budget while the guys discussed sports. We all had so much in common, we were more like a family than friendly acquaintances. There were few secrets among us. News traveled fast. In fact, it didn't have far to go. The thin walls were little more than sight barriers, so private conversations in one apartment soon became public property. We always knew who was having the next baby before the parents were ready to announce it to the world.

Children were everywhere! When we moved in, John commented that it looked like the "shoe" of Mother Goose fame. Several couples had been there for two or three years and had already started families. We soon realized that the village wasn't called Fertile Valley without reason.

From the moment John walked on the field, it was apparent that he was the "big man" on campus. He made every play with the tenacity of a vicious bulldog, never letting up. Because of his quickness, he seemed to be everywhere at once. The coaches liked him for that, and his fellow athletes liked him for his team play and will to win. My former classmates from high school thought it must be wonderful to be the wife of a superstar football player. I told myself how lucky I was to be in the center of all this adulation, but deep down inside me a gnawing sense of doubt was beginning to grow. It wasn't exactly the way I had pictured it.

From the beginning, I had labored under the illusion that I would be able to make John over into a man just like my father. We would have this wonderful sports career, with all the money we could spend, enjoying the best of everything. I wasn't ready to give up on my dream, but I could see that for the immediate future, it would require revision.

One day as I was walking across campus after work, one of the wives from the village caught up with me. I had met her, but didn't know much about her. I thought she was cute and a snappy dresser, but we had never really had a conversation. It was one of those soft, last days of summer when the breeze has just enough cooling in it to keep you outside. Reluctant to go inside when we reached the apartments, I suggested we go for a coke. It was the beginning of a friendship that still keeps us close.

As Linda Parish and I sat under a tree and talked, I realized how much I needed someone I could share my thoughts with, just the random hopes and dreams that often come to nothing. The honest thoughts that may or may not be important tomorrow. The kinds of ideas that husbands and wives often share. If they have the time and interest.

John and I talked; he could talk about sports for hours, and so could I. It was our life. And our hope for the future. In those times when everything was going well, I was happy. What we never talked about was his behavior. At least, not for long. Any mention of his misconduct, and I immediately found myself in the center of an erupting volcano of anger.

I knew John drank before I married him. I think I saw it as something that he did with his friends that had nothing to do with our lives. I am sure I thought it would present no future problems. And we would be so happy and content in our own home that he would feel no need for anything that didn't include me.

What I didn't know was his dark side. That unreasoning rage that seemed aimed at destroying everything in its path. Through all the times we were together before marriage, he was considerate and thoughtful; always attentive to my feelings. Suddenly, I was thrown into a fearful maze of verbal abuse I would never have believed existed. In my home, nothing like this had ever happened.

The first time John came home drunk was an initiation to my immediate future. Before the door closed he was unleashing the full force of a caustic anger on me; an anger that changed his entire appearance. I stared at him in shock, then tried to soothe his aggression by reaching out to him. He roughly slapped me out of his way, glaring at me as if I were a stranger. When my tears welled up and spilled over, it only angered him more.

"Little Miss Perfect," he sneered. "What makes you so great! Mama's little angel has everything all planned the way she wants it— well, that ain't the way it's gonna be! You're in the real world now! You're gonna be livin' like real people!"

Shoving me against the wall, he yelled, "I'll be calling the shots around here—you got that?"

I was heartbroken. Not so much at the words as the look on his face. He looked as if he didn't care whether I lived or died. I might have been a little better prepared for his tirades had I known more about his home life, and the kind of male behavior to which he had been accustomed. Instead, each time it happened, I wondered what I had said or done to set him off. I was convinced that it was my fault when things went wrong. I was desperate for him to know that nothing could ever change my love for him, that we could solve all the problems by calmly talking through them. Had I dared evaluate the success of that attitude, I would have seen the hopelessness of the situation. He rejected any form of criticism, so I quickly learned to cushion every word with caution.

I knew the other couples in our building could hear every word spoken because his voice went up several decibels when he was drinking. I was too ashamed to talk to anyone about it. Somehow in my mind I reasoned that every problem has a solution, and it was up to me to find it. If, as John often yelled, everything was my fault, I could figure out what I was doing wrong and stop it. I still had enough pride in my own strength to believe I could somehow prove to John that he needed to change. I often wavered between this attitude and utter hopelessness.

Only once did I feel so utterly alone and without hope, that I gave up. John had physically hurt me on that occasion; pulling out a handful of hair and banging my head against the wall. As I tried to analyze my situation, I realized how tired I was of the struggle. *Why had I been so hasty? What had I done to myself? What could I do now? I needed my mother!*

Before I could change my mind, I went home. Once there, I became defensive of John enough to ease up on the graphic details of his abuse. I'm sure my mother had no idea of the seriousness of our situation. I could see her reluctance to take sides, not wanting to align herself against either. She finally told me my place was now with my husband; that marriage was not something to take lightly.

She let me know that I needed to honor those vows; that I needed to try harder.

With her limited information of what our married life was like, I knew she was giving the best advice she could. And I was responsible for where I was; nobody had coerced me into it. Lying in the bed I made for myself may well have been what I deserved, but telling myself that fact didn't make it any easier.

When John punched his fist through a wall, or smashed a table, or threw a chair across the room, it drew no more than a glance from me. I was only too glad to see the furniture go flying instead of me. The many times he punched his fist into me, or twisted my arm, or slammed me against the wall, I just tried to quietly endure it till he stopped and threw me aside. Sometimes he only bellowed obscenities at me but even that, like physical blows, left me cowering in a corner.

It never occurred to me to seek help again. I couldn't confide in friends or family for fear it would be construed as an admission that I'd made a bad mistake and was unwilling to accept the consequences of my error in judgment. I just hid all my dread and worry behind a smiling facade and continued my silence.

Going to the out-of-town games with the girls was an experience I approached with mixed emotion. On the one hand, the carefree chatter between us was fun and a release to me of some of the frustration I was feeling. On the other, I could never completely let go of the tension for fear someone might ask me something personal I didn't want to answer. I just glued my little smiley face on and pretended I was as happy as the rest of them. And in some strange way I really was at times.

It was impossible not to catch the contagious excitement in the stands on those golden Saturday afternoons. It caught you at the first roar of the crowd. With the crisp autumn air crackling around you carrying thousands of vibrant voices screaming, "KILL, BRAMLETT, KILL," that moment was all that mattered.

I'm sure those games were better for me than I knew. All my tension drained away in that atmosphere. John was a home crowd pleaser, Memphis State's ideal of what a football player should be. Tough and mean, asking no quarter and giving none. One of the homecoming floats in his sophomore year used his jersey number on a blown-up facsimile of the MSU Tiger mascot. As the float rolled by in the parade, the strains of "Big Bad John," boomed out. Although he was not so big as a football player at less than two hundred pounds, I could have told them the term "Bad," was a perfect fit!

Getting so much attention did nothing to settle him down. He acted as if he owned the place. He was the drinking companion of choice for all the students who liked rubbing elbows with a sports hero. He was the unquestioned leader of campus mischief, too but leading "panty raids," went beyond schoolboy pranks to me. I felt compelled to stand up and be counted on that one.

"John," I began, "How could you do that? How do you think that makes me feel? You, a married man, sneaking into the women's dorm to steal their underwear! It is humiliating to me."

For once, instead of throwing a mad fit, he laughed and taunted me with being jealous. He kept it going as long as he could, as if he had done something really clever. I had to admit to myself, *of course I was jealous*, but I wasn't about to let him know it.

It was just his typical way of never missing an opportunity to publicly embarrass me. Pushing me aside or belittling me in front of others kept me off balance, and made me feel insignificant. At such times, I wondered how we had come to this. When I felt that I couldn't take any more, I would try to gather enough courage to try to appeal to him through another venue.

"John, everyone is proud of the way you play, and I think Coach Murphy really appreciates what you do for the team."

"Yeah, I know," he quickly agreed.

I then *carefully* pointed out that the coach was building a football team to make Memphis State proud, and that *John* was an essential part of it. I then would very tactfully mention that no one was so essential that he wouldn't be kicked off the team if his actions became an embarrassment to the college. My subtle warning had no effect. John set his own proprieties; he was *Somebody* at last, and he did as he pleased.

He wore this attitude like a banner. If I could see it, so could others, and that thought gave me many sleepless nights. Every place he went, he could almost always be counted on to start a rousing fight, and when he was out drinking, I was afraid to answer the phone for fear it was the police. He became very good at listening for approaching sirens, managing to extricate himself in time to escape before the officers arrived.

———»•«———

A week or so before Thanksgiving, I awoke one morning to an urgency to get to the bathroom quickly. After about ten minutes of heaving to expel everything in my stomach, I stood blinking dazedly at the wall. The staggering thought hit me squarely in the face: *I was pregnant!*

For once, John was ecstatic with me. He boasted to his buddies about the son who was going to follow in his tracks and be just like him. *God forbid, I prayed silently.*

For the first time in our married life, he became solicitous of me, and I was basking happily in what I had hoped for from the beginning. When the bruises all faded, I hoped the memories of the beatings would disappear as well. For the most part they did, but I sometimes would awaken from sleep in a cold sweat with the specter of a hard fist smashing into me.

John still drank heavily, but he was careful to direct his senseless antagonism at others. When Andy was born in July of 1961, I felt rewarded for all the misery I had gone through. *I knew I would gladly do it all over again for this beautiful baby boy!*

Miraculously, John seemed more at peace with everything for a while—only for a while. Now, instead of tormenting me, he just stayed away. Never there unless it was absolutely necessary, he was completely indifferent to everything at home except the baby. He was obsessed with Andy's growth rate. He wanted him to get old enough overnight to start learning to play ball. He talked constantly about how they would do everything together. He was a very attentive dad when he was there, and I was beginning to translate that into the much hoped for "good father" image.

A year later, in 1962, our second son, Don was born. I had suffered such a long, hard labor bringing Andy into the world, I was totally unprepared for the quick delivery of Don. Forty-five minutes after I entered the hospital, our second son was regaling the hospital staff loudly with proof of his strong lungs.

It was easier to forget my fears of the future when I looked into the faces of those two little boys. If any power on earth could give John a sense of responsibility, I knew it would be his sons.

~ *Chapter Four* ~

When I became a mother, all the other wives with children rallied around to help me. Someone was always there with motherly advice affecting everything from baby's ear infections to potty training. My mother and dad adored their grandsons, and offered help with everything. After being lost in a wilderness of uncertainty for so long, I felt overwhelmed by so much attention. I had come to terms with the consequences of my hasty decision to marry John by using my deep-seated love for him as a gauge; if the day ever came when my unreasoning love for him was gone, I would follow.

The tenderness I'd cherished in our dating days had vanished long ago. His only concern was having his needs met; that accomplished, he indifferently went his way. Our physical contact gave me little satisfaction; if I clung to him a moment too long, it angered him. He seemed to see every overture I made as censure. He never learned to accept any form of disapproval. To John, there was no such thing as constructive criticism.

Andy and Don became my reasons for living, providing the energy I needed to face whatever crisis John brought on us for the day. I was constantly repeating a metamorphosis of hope that either John would see what he was doing to us and change, or that I would suffer a tragic accident that would enable me to give up and go home to stay forever. Anything to save me from this life of constant turmoil. I found that I could barely remember how it felt to have control of my own feelings.

When the fall semester of John's senior year began, we decided I should quit my job and be at home with the boys full time. For once we were in complete agreement, and suddenly, I was having the most fun I had ever had! I loved getting together with all the other young mothers with their babies and toddlers. We swapped stories about every cute thing our children did, and compared notes from all the child-care books.

In spite of the lurking apprehension always over-shadowing every day, my little boys were helping me develop a new resolve to make the most of my life. I refused to dwell on the unpleasant incidents that showed up with alarming regularity. I shielded Andy and Don from them as much as possible.

In spite of John's reputation, he could turn on the charm and convince people that he was Mr. Nice Guy when he wanted something. In his senior year, he was captain of the football team. He was then elected Mr. Memphis State, voted in by the student body. No one other than a fraternity member had ever won. Suddenly John was becoming more pleasant. Less combative. I think the prestigious title   of Mr. Memphis State, singling him out as representative of the college, gave him the self esteem he needed.

We've turned the corner, I thought. With graduation only days away, I was feeling the excitement of anticipation of a future that closely resembled the dreams we had when we first met. Life was changing, I could feel it. I could see a bright horizon of promise opening up before us. Thankfully, our sight is limited to the horizon instead of what waits beyond it.

When a scout from the Saint Louis Cardinals' baseball organization, Buddy Lewis, came to our apartment to offer John a contract, he gave him an $ 8,000 bonus for signing.

I knew John would have preferred to play football, but all the pro scouts who interviewed him told him he was too small to make it in their league.

John was informed by the Cardinals that after graduation, he would be going to Winnipeg, Canada, to play for the St. Louis farm team. We agreed that the boys and I should stay in Memphis until he got a chance to play on one of their teams closer to home. Nothing was going to dampen our enthusiasm, not with $ 8,000 in our hands. We rented a beautiful apartment with two bedrooms, near the Mid-South Fairgrounds, and wasted no time moving in. We replaced the old Nash car that my dad had given us with a shining new Chevrolet. That little Nash had always reminded me of a beetle scuttling around, but it was tough as a tank. Now that we were in the money, I was only too happy to leave those Vets Village days behind us.

Everywhere we went in Memphis, John was the center of attention. I reveled in his limelight, feeling almost like a celebrity myself Just when I was starting to get my own self-esteem back, John tripped me up again. It was graduation day, and all of our family members were there to celebrate it with him. After the festivities ended, John insisted that I take the boys home. When I hesitated to go without him, he assured me he would be right there behind us.

He did not show up at home until very late the next day. I was furious; how could he do this to me? Nobody had sacrificed more, nobody had worked harder for his success than I! I asked myself, what do you do in the face of such total disregard for your feelings? I'd tried patience, I'd tried kindness, I'd tried begging nothing had helped! The more I thought, the more worked up I became. By the time he walked in the door, I was ready to fight back.

When he hardly glanced at me before walking right past me, I picked up the first thing I saw and hurled it at him as hard as I could. It happened to be his treasured Humes High captain's trophy. The shining, football player statue lost its head when it hit the wall with all the force of my attack. Its decapitated head rolled across the floor and under the bed. A severed arm and a leg lay a few feet away.

"How do you like that?" I taunted. "Maybe that will get your attention! Look at it! That's what I'd like to do to you! It's what you deserve!"

He stared at me with fire in his eyes. Not sure what he might do, I decided I'd gone far enough. I quickly picked up Don and left the room. John went into the bathroom and showered as if nothing had happened. I payed for that lapse in my passive resistance for a very long time. Even after I apologized over and over, he held on to a resentful sulk.

When I couldn't take it any longer, I took the pieces of his broken trophy over to a trophy shop near the college and asked the proprietor if he could repair it. He promised to do what he could. I could see how curious he was, but I offered no explanation for its condition.

I knew I had gone too far. I was sure John was plotting to get even in some way I would find painful. When I went to see about the trophy, it looked so good it might have just been presented When I showed it to John, he just shrugged his shoulders as if it meant nothing to him. But I noticed that his disposition did improve.

I had long ago learned that patient acceptance of his bad behavior brought no rewards. Angry recriminations were forthcoming from him, whatever approach I took. Knowing he would soon be on a plane to join the Cardinals' Northern League Farm Club in Winnipeg, I tried to be hopeful and happy. I got a large group of relatives and friends together at the airport to see him off. Watching all the hugs, handshakes and slaps on the back,

Grandchildren are the crowning glory.
Proverbs 17:6

Rebecca "Puddin" • Nancy • Rachel "Punkin"
Hunter "Pistol" • John "Bull" • Jordan "Pro"

The loves of my life.

Can two walk together,
except they be agreed?
Amos 3:3

John and Nancy

Children are a heritage from the Lord
Psalms 127:3

John · Hunter · Rebecca · Nancy · Jordan · Rachel

A friend loveth at all times
Proverbs 17:17

Nancy (Ethel)
and Linda (Lucy) Parish

A merry heart doeth
good like a medicine.

Proverbs 17:22

I convinced myself that now he would see things differently; now he would develop the maturity to act responsibly.

That was a joke! Even though I was in Memphis, stories began filtering back to me from Winnipeg. Stories about broken curfews, and fires set on buses carrying players from city to city. Of feet-first plays that broke jaws and noses, and knocked out teeth. Opposing teams objected to John's "anything goes" style of play, lending to the ugly confrontations that often erupted on the field. The adolescent pranks, the questionable plays, and his drinking and fighting continued unabated.

I was glad to be in Memphis. At least I was finding some semblance of a peaceful life near people who cared for my boys and me. John called often, usually after their games. On one particularly happy occasion, he had made a grand slam. It was a game which gave him the nickname that stuck: "Bull." Someone on the opposing team had hit a fly ball toward John's position at third base and he had taken off running for it, full speed. Afterward, giving me a blow-by-blow account, he said, "I knew there was a fence along the left field sideline, but I wasn't about to take my eyes off the ball. I charged through that fence and made the catch. When I came back out where I'd crashed through, my face was bleeding, but all I was feeling was that ball in my glove! Someone in the home stands yelled something about a charging bull, and the crowd took up the chant: "Bull, Bull, Bull!"

After that episode hit the newspapers, John became "Bull" Bramlett for life. I ruefully agreed that it suited him perfectly. He had snorted and stomped and pawed his way through whatever dared confront him up to now.

He always liked to give me a play-by-play account of his good games, and basking in his good mood, I never mentioned all the rumors floating back to me. I knew if he sensed my displeasure, he just wouldn't call me, so I never said anything to upset him. When my attitude made him feel especially good, I could expect a big bouquet of red roses, so a local florist made many deliveries to my house.

As the end of the season approached, I was feeling mixed emotions about his return home. I didn't know anything to do but what I always had; just do what I could to keep peace, and hang on to my sanity!

Just prior to Thanksgiving, a world-shaking tragedy brought sadness to the home of every American. The entire nation was shocked out of any sense of complacency by the shared nightmare of President John F. Kennedy's assassination. The enormity of it made the world seem less safe, and ordinary day-to-day living less simple. For a brief time, it even seemed to have a sobering effect on John's attitude. As pictures of the vulnerable, grieving widow and two small children flashed around the world, we all felt personally wounded. It awakened in me a disturbing uncertainty that refused to go away.

Questioning my own sense of fairness was a new experience for me. I had believed implicitly in my standard of values because it was my heritage. My parents lived a well-ordered life, so it was my model of excellence. What if I had been born into a different family, like John's, for instance? Would I, too, have a different personality? It was a possibility from which my thoughts would not let me escape.

What I had learned of John's family had come mostly from his own drunken raving. I knew he idolized his older brothers, and felt protective of his younger brother, Bobby. I knew he respected his mother. I learned early on that any thought of his father could set him off like a firecracker. I got the distinct impression that his father ruled with an iron fist, and was very "Religious." John always spoke of religion like that, with great emphasis on it, as if it were a dirty word. I took it to mean that he didn't care much for "Religion!"

I'd heard enough to know the Bramlett men made all the decisions. I knew they drank, that it was considered a part of becoming a man in a man's world. All of this I heard from John. The rest I would learn from association.

In those times when I was trying desperately to understand the man I had married, I tormented myself with feelings of guilt. *Why hadn't I been willing to wait till we were older! And more settled!*

Those times of self-doubt always ended in the same way, serving only to immerse me in one deeply troubling memory from the past. Most of John's unrestrained fits of anger started out with growled insults and accusations, moving on to shouted obscenities directed at me. I could never learn what to do or say to appease him; the harder I tried, the worse it got. If he stumbled over a chair, it was because I deliberately put it there to trip him up. If I spoke a word in defense of myself, he was all over me with an open-handed slap or a shove.

The time that left an indelible scar on my memory also left me with the fear that I would one day die at his hands. He had roughly shoved me backward on the bed. As I lay crumpled in a heap crying, he suddenly straddled me and clenched his hands around my throat. As the air was cut off to my lungs, I began frantically struggling to break his strangle hold. As my strength ebbed away, everything faded into blackness around me. I guess he came to his senses enough to let go of me, for I was choking and coughing and gulping air when his face came into focus.

The dark bruises left by his hands slowly faded from my neck, but the scars to my heart clung unforgettably for many years. I carefully covered my neck with scarves while my throat healed.

After this happened, John's physical abuse became noticeably less severe. When he was angry, he satisfied his ugly moods with yelling and sulking. When he wasn't drinking, he was more like the man I fell in love with. From the day I saw him, I could not imagine being with any other man, even in the worst of times. When he was sober, I learned to live in the moment. When he lapsed into his old ways, I just held on and waited it out. I buried my head in the sand, and refused to think too far ahead. I couldn't have said that I thought he would eventually change nothing indicated that; I only knew that I was not ready to give up on him. I think I convinced myself that it's always too soon to quit.

.

~ Chapter Five ~

I watch as he opens the official looking envelope with the Cardinals' insignia in the corner. The contents are blunt, straight-forward, and conclusive. After careful consideration of his impact on the team, his services are no longer required due to his undisciplined behavior and inability to adapt to management, his contract with the St. Louis Cardinals' Minor League System will not be renewed. John is finished. Washed up. It is over.

He hands me the letter and leaves the apartment without a word. I know where he is going. The place he always goes when things go swimmingly, or sour. The place he goes when he is up, or down. To the nearest liquor store. I wait I give the boys their supper, bathe them and put them to bed. And I wait.

I know he will be late. And drunk. Very late and very, very drunk

My mother was a cheerful optimist with a ready smile and a strong sense of humor. My dad, loving and kind, was perfect for her. I suppose I had thought that somehow, such things were inherited. Growing up, my plan was to have a marriage just like theirs. The family teasingly called me "Miss Scarlett," because of my conviction in every situation that if I looked cute enough I could handle any-thing. If today should turn out to be a bust, there was always tomorrow, and "tomorrow was another day."

Waking up in what was left of our apartment the morn-ing after John received his career ending notice from the Cards was sickening. I could hardly bear to look at the wreckage. It was not unexpected; I just hadn't known any way to stop it. There was hardly a piece of furniture still standing. He had completely smashed everything in sight. The only untouched room was the bedroom in which the boys slept.

When he grabbed the coffee table by a leg to sling it across the room, all the objects on it went flying. I had set a cup of coffee on it just moments before, hoping he would drink it and settle down. The entire cup spilled on the sofa, sending an ugly, brown stain all the way across it. As long as we lived in the apartment, that stain was a silent reminder of his rampage against convention. His lifelong dream was dead, and he was mourning it in the only way he knew. I actually feared for his life. He drank a whole pint of whiskey, straight, while I pleaded with him to stop.

Suddenly he crouched into a three-point stance as if in a football line. Charging hard, he ran at full speed toward the end of the living room. When he hit the wall, he crashed through to the kitchen side as if the sheetrock and plaster had been paper. His head had missed a two-by-four stud by about an inch. Seeing how close he came to breaking his neck seemed to drain some of the violence out of him.

Hard, wrenching sobs racked his body. I could no more have helped what I did next than I could have helped comforting Andy or Don. I held him in my arms, and cried with him. Blood from a cut on his head mingled with our tears and ran down his tormented face.

"Sh-h-h," I crooned soothingly; "It's going to be all right, you'll see, everything will look better tomorrow. Let's get your clothes off and let you get some sleep." He let me guide him into the bedroom. He didn't resist as I helped him get undressed. After cleaning the cut on his head and putting antiseptic on it, I managed to get him to the bed. Still muttering incoherently, he finally passed out.

Thank the Lord, I sighed in relief. I stood there for several minutes just gazing down at him. Lying there quietly, he looked like a lost little boy. The rush of tenderness and love I felt for this man was totally beyond my comprehension.

With neither the inclination nor energy to start cleaning up the shambles John had made of the apartment, I just turned out the lights and got into bed.

———•◦•———

Opening my eyes to a ray of sunlight through the loosely drawn blinds, I quickly showered and dressed. I felt driven to restore some semblance of order before John got up to face what he had done. Soon after I started picking up and taking out the clutter of broken chairs, dishes and furniture, I looked up to see him standing in the doorway watching me. In an instant he had me in his arms with my head buried in his chest.

"Nancy, Nancy, what have I done? How did I do all this? You shouldn't even see something like this, much less be cleaning it up." For once, he seemed sincerely contrite.

I was thinking ahead, wondering how I could conceal the mess from anyone who happened to come by, especially Mom and Dad. *I'll get the maintenance man in first thing, and figure out a way to keep people away from here for a day or two.*

The more John hung around the apartment moping, the more edgy I became. I wanted to say, "John, you did this you brought it on yourself," but I didn't. I was angry with him one minute for putting us all in this position then forgiving the next moment, because he never seemed to realize what he was doing wrong.

I fell into the habit of beginning every day with the same routine: thinking up new ideas for encouraging John. *Stay in touch with the people you know in pro sports. Call Mr. Stanky up... he always liked you and tried to help you whenever he*

could. Don't let yourself go —keep your body in shape. For all you
know, some NFL football team may be looking for a linebacker.

Eddie Stanky was in charge of the minor league system
for the Cardinals, and had been instrumental in keeping
John out of jail on several occasions. After one of them,
I wrote Mr. Stanky a letter thanking him for giving John
another chance. I poured out my heart to this man I had
met only briefly. I tried to explain to him the circumstances
that I believed contributed to John's irrational behavior;
I also told him how much I appreciated his believing in
John's potential enough to help him.

Years later in a chance meeting, he told me that he had
kept my letter. He said my defense of John, and my devo-
tion to him had touched him deeply. Mr. Stanky, a family
man himself, knew the difficulties of family life in the
professional sports world, and didn't want to see our
marriage become another casualty.

We had stayed in touch enough to know that Eddie
Stanky was currently with the Mets, so John called him
there. His old mentor was cautious, not exactly optimistic,
but he didn't slam the door either on someone he must
have known was grasping at straws.

Although my words about a linebacker proved pro-
phetic, I wouldn't have believed it at the time. I was just
trying to fan a flicker of hope in John.

A few days after John's call to Mr. Stanky, we got a
phone call from Ray Malavasi. He was John's former
coach at MSU. When he said he was in Memphis and
would like to see us, John invited him over. He had moved
on to Denver as a defensive coach for the Broncos. He told
John he was in town to do some scouting, and thought
about him. He was looking at several MSU players,
primarily for tough, hard-hitting linebackers.

After they went through their back-slapping cama-
raderie, Ray opened up and told John that he was
actually there to offer him a chance, just a chance, to make
the football team for the coming season. "You have the
ability, John," he urged him. "All you lack is the weight.
If you want to take a shot at it, I think I can help you. I'll
lay out a stringent program of training for you to follow.
It won't be easy; it's absolutely essential for you to get your
weight up to 220 pounds "

"Coach, I'll do anything for a chance to play pro football.
You know how I love it. I don't care how hard it is."

"John, it won't come easy. You'll have to build strength
and develop stamina, too; not just bulk and weight."

"I know! I know! I can do it, Coach."

"Not so fast," Malavasi interrupted. "You haven't heard
everything. And this is the most important part. There are
only six months before tryouts. During those six months
there will be no booze and no tobacco. You will eat what
I tell you. You will work out when I tell you, for as long as
I tell you, and do it the way I tell you. Do you still think
you can do it?"

"Coach, I can do it! I'm ready to start now! Let's get
it going!"

I couldn't remember when I'd seen John so excited. *Pro
football! His dream from when I'd first met him. And even though
he had seemingly been forced to give up on it, here was hope in
another chance!* I realized we had yet to face the reality of
making the team, but it was worth taking the chance.
What did we have to lose? I could see that I was going to
have to lay myself on the line for this to work. It would
require my efforts, too, in preparing the right kind of
meals, and pushing when he tired of the routine. In a
strange way, it was my chance, too; my chance to make
John see my importance to him. I felt, deep in my heart, a

stirring of hope, not only for John in a career he wanted, but hope for a better life for our sons. And for myself.

Talk about a life-changing event, in one half-hour, we had gone from looking down a dark tunnel of sheer despair, to nothing but sunshine and crackerjacks! We were ecstatic!

Somewhere in the back of my mind, a lingering thought of Ray's warning about alcohol kept nagging at me. I would believe that part of the training when I saw it! I needn't have worried. From the moment Coach Malavasi left our apartment, John went into immediate, total training. With pit bull tenacity, he set up his own training program before he even received the instructions from Denver. Every waking moment was concentrated on achieving his goal. Behind his back, acquaintances had negative things to say. *Why doesn't he quit chasing a dream? It's time for him to grow up and get real! Everything is just a game to Bramlett. He needs to get a real job!*

To us, it was anything but playing a game. It was hard work, and we were in it for the long haul. John was not about to give up. Neither was I. I think I would have died before quitting. The cavalier attitude of *our song* had deserted us, swallowed up in our new resolve.

John was stone sober for the first time in longer than I could remember. He had stopped drinking, fighting, smoking, chewing tobacco, and staying out late. For the first time in our marriage I was living with a model husband. Andy and Don were learning how much fun their dad could be. And I was hopelessly, irretrievably, in love again with this man who had taught me to trust no one.

We were living the home life I had always imagined. And the most wonderful part about it was that John seemed happiest of all.

~ *Chapter Six* ~

In my typical *Miss Scarlett* persona, I knew before the six months training was finished that we had reached our goal. I kept John so full of steak and potatoes, and every other form of protein, starch and carbohydrates available, that he was tipping the scales at about two-eighteen with three weeks to go.

I had begun dreading his departure date. The boys and I settled down to remain in Memphis while we waited to see if he made the team. For the first time in our life together, we were actually sharing things, leaning on each other, and all of a sudden, I couldn't bear to give it up. He had desperately needed me during this training period, and now I was being left behind. On the way to the airport, I tried to mirror his happy optimism, but my heart was sinking into my shoes.

"Don't worry, honey, you'll be out there before you know it! Just pack your bags and get ready!" His words told me that at least, I was hiding my frustration reasonably well.

Neither of us would admit to the slightest hint of doubt that he would make the team. It was just a matter of getting the money together to make the move! Hugging and kissing the boys, he told them, "It snows a lot in Denver, and we'll get out and make the biggest snowman you ever saw, right up on top of those Rocky Mountains."

Our family members were all there to see him off. All the handshakes, back slapping, and good wishes had John laughing, but I couldn't seem to keep my eyes dry. We had worked hard for this, but as he turned to me for that last goodbye kiss, I felt a chill go through me. In that moment, I felt that the closeness we had known for the past six months was over, never to return.

———»•«———

Week after week, as John survived the cut—Mom, Dad and I breathed a little easier. When he called to say he had made the final cut that made him a Bronco, our happiness knew no bounds. And when we set out across country to Denver, Mom and Dad decided to go along to help with Andy and Don. We left town like a modern-day bunch of gypsies traveling in a caravan.

It was hardly a fun trip. The boys were tired and hot, and hated being restricted so long in the car. They wore us all out. After the monotony of driving across the plains, I've never forgotten the excitement of topping a sloping eleva-tion in the road to see the Rockies rising majestically before us. The clear, clean air of Colorado's Mile-High city quickly revived our high spirits.

With so many willing hands to help, we were quickly settled into a comfortable apartment and ready for the first home game. On game day, I was so thrilled, I must have gone to the stadium two hours before game time. I still remember how my heart was pounding at the kickoff. *John's very first professional football game!* Television cameras seemed to be everywhere, filming the game.

From the moment the Broncos ran onto the field, all I could see was John. Smiling in anticipation and satisfac-tion, I was caught full face on camera as it swept the crowd of players' wives. Mama Lotta, watching at home, saw me. From then on, she expected to see me every time John's team was televised. I didn't have the heart to explain to her that I was not the main attraction.

All the hoopla of that first day carried me for a few games, but not for long. John had assumed his former "anything goes," attitude almost immediately after making the team. If anything, he was meaner than ever, more arrogant. His wild antics were written up for the sports news as if he were a hero, which didn't help. I was proud of his play on the field, but he had added pill popping to his drinking, and this seemed to make him even more violent.

I began to wonder how long he would last in professional sports with his present style of living. He refused to accept the limitations of his body and often played in games hurting from previous injuries. With tears streaming down my face, I would plead with him, "John, please tell the Coach about this pain you're in, he'll understand. If you'd miss one game, you could heal!" He'd just shake me off and growl, "I gotta go, Nancy," and be out the door.

I was amazed at what appeared to be an unwritten law in professional sports. With the exception of murder, whatever the favored athletes did seemed not only accepted, but applauded. Adultery simply added another notch to a player's esteem. In retrospect, I know there must have been some fine young men there who honored the rules of conventionality, but somehow they're the ones we don't hear about. While I worried, John became one of the more popular athletes around the city. Because of his growing reputation for being the toughest linebacker in sports, much of what he did while drunk was ignored by the local police.

The other sports wives were very supportive to newcomers. I quickly formed friendships that have lasted through the years. I think we found in each other a common meeting ground of empathy that allowed us to express our feelings without betrayal of our fierce loyalties to our husbands. When our guys practiced or played, we all got together for whatever was planned.

Mary Malavasi was a mother-figure for all of us. With five children, she had the credentials. She was a warm, generous, loving woman who guided us through many troubled times with softly spoken encouragement.

One cold, rainy day when we were all together, a light bulb went off in Jo An Lee's head. Jo An's husband was the Bronco quarterback, Jacky Lee.

"Let me tell you what we did in Buffalo," she said. "On days like this, we had the greatest thing going! Jack Kemp's wife, Joanne, started a social club where we could develop our individual talents. We did all kinds of things: some were just simple crafts like fabric painting and collages. We learned how to do ceramics, rug-hooking, the whole bit. It was fun! We could do something like that here."

To be actually accomplishing something in these hours we enjoyed together was a great idea After that, we began planning our meetings, keeping each other's children, exchanging recipes, doing crafts, and helping each other with simple home emergencies. Sometimes we shopped together in teams, then all met for lunch. On out of town game days, we gathered at one location to watch and cheer our team on.

I came to depend so much on those times, I wondered if anyone else was as desperate for support as I felt. Always, in the back of my mind was the fear of change, the fear that John would do something to cause him to be thrown off the team, or be injured to the point of being unable to play. My world had shrunk to the football field and all that emanated from it.

When the year was over, we packed up and went home for the off-season. We had decided to buy a house so we could put our roots down in the familiar soil of Memphis. What a great move it turned out to be! My friend, Linda, from our Memphis State days, and her husband, Paul, lived just a block from the house we bought. We had stayed in touch through the years, getting together for lunch whenever I was in Memphis. Now that we would be living near them, my dream of permanent roots became even sweeter!

My confidence was suddenly soaring! So was John's; he was offered an off-season job with Dixiemart Carondolet as their consultant for uniforms, and for all baseball, softball, basketball and football equipment. He was happy getting to spend time talking about sports, and signing autographs like a celebrity, which of course, he was. He was *my celebrity!*

In those all-too-brief months of summer in our new home, I was working hard to establish a pattern of stability. Having our own home had awakened in me an even greater sense of responsibility for Andy and Don. They were now coming up on five and four, and showing signs of John's impulsive aggressiveness. My dad was invaluable in those years of their early development. He adored them and spent all the time he could with them. As John was seldom at home, he thought it was wonder-ful for Dad to be so devoted to them, though his reasons were far different to mine. I was hoping for Dad's gentle ways to rub off on them.

I was seeing all I could of Linda. Her husband, Paul, worked for the FAA on the swing shift, so if at home, he was usually sleeping. I'm sure John's lifestyle, which accounted for his constant absence from home, must have been incomprehensible to Paul Parish. Paul seemed to like nothing better than having their son, Jeff, with him, and they were always happy to include Andy and Don. Later, when our boys were in school, Linda and I did a lot of volunteer work for PTA and special projects.

The oasis of our friendship became a steadying influence in my life. Linda was one of those outgoing people who seemed to find her perfect place to fit in, wherever she went. She always managed to *see* what was there to see. Consequently, I imagine she saw a lot more of my real need than I realized at the time. She and Paul had been friends with my family since MSU days, so they were included when we all got together. We were a large, loud and loving group and those times together were the only times in which I could relax in the peace I longed for.

Not wanting to seem disloyal to John, I was careful around family members to avoid mention of anything that he said or did that bothered me. I soon learned that with Linda, I could let off steam in indirect ways without calling names or getting in over my head. While our children played around our feet, we carried on a running commentary about the "characters" in the latest drama without them having a clue about what was actually being discussed. We understood each other's thoughts and feelings so well, we sometimes finished each other's sentences. In the same manner we still often pick up on a conversation that started years before, and know immediately that we are on the same page.

As our first summer drew to a close after one season with the Broncos, we began to prepare to return to Denver. Surprisingly, I found myself looking forward to going. I was determined to become more of an influence in John's life by convincing him to spend more of his time with the boys. He was so appreciative of my dad's time with them. I had already begun my campaign to strengthen the ties between John and his sons. His love for them was never in question; they were his favorite topic everywhere he went.

Just before we closed the house for departure, John met Joe Namath at a Pro-Am Golf Tournament in Memphis. I knew Joe was a hero to John, so I took Andy and Don out to the Colonial Country Club where they were playing. Joe was so nice and the boys were crazy about him. When play ended, we took Joe over to meet Dad and Mother. Before he left, he had a promise from me to cook dinner for him on his next trip to Denver. John had bragged that I was famous for my Southern fried chicken, mashed potatoes, gravy and biscuits.

True to our promise, when the Jets came to town, we invited Joe over. We could not have had more delightful dinner guests than Joe and his teammate, Ray Abruzzi. We all laughed and joked the evening away over a dinner of all I had promised, and more. Joe's favorite thing was my green bean casserole, and he insisted that I tell him step-by-step how I did it. Long before the evening ended, we felt as if we had known them for years. That dinner together was one of many that we continued to share in our home with Joe, but come Sunday afternoon when the cameras started rolling, he and John became formidable opposing forces.

Many of John's football buddies loved hearing his stories about growing up in Memphis, especially the ones including Elvis. John, his brothers and Elvis Presley were from the same neighborhood and had grown up together. They had remained good friends.

John was several years younger than Elvis, but he always trotted along behind the older boys, so they accepted his presence. John was small, but made up for it in toughness, so he soon became a favorite when they played one of Elvis' famous tag football games. After he grew up, Elvis followed John's career, and affectionately called him "Little Bramlett."

After becoming famous, Elvis never forgot his friends from the old neighborhood. He stayed in touch when he could, and occasionally called up to try getting a group together for touch football. I think John and Elvis felt a special bond because both had come from North Memphis and had "made it" professionally. Neither was interested in trying to impress each other or anyone else; they just appreciated how far they had come. Over the years, many times when the phone rang, it was a message from Elvis inviting us over to Graceland for breakfast and a game. Some of the time it was late afternoon and almost time for dinner. That never bothered Elvis; when he got up hungry, it was time for breakfast.

As it became harder for him to have any privacy outside his home, he would sometimes rent the old Memphian theater on Cooper Street, and invite a group to share a movie with him. It was on such an occasion that we first met Priscilla. I remember being struck by how young and pretty she was, and I couldn't help thinking how hard it was going to be for them to ever have any kind of settled life together.

~ *Chapter Seven* ~

My high hopes for John's second season were shattered in their first regular season game when he made a flying tackle and came down awkwardly on his left shoulder. I could tell he was in intense pain as he came off the field, but after shots of novocaine and cortisone, he went back in. He went the entire season doped up and taped up, with badly torn muscles in his shoulder.

After what others saw as a good season for him, John was again voted to the Pro-Bowl. I knew what it had cost him. I could even make excuses to myself for his bad temper. I could overlook his excessive indulgence in pain-killers and alcohol, but I was becoming fearful that it was all going to catch up with him.

It was such a relief when the season ended and we could go home and check John into Campbell Clinic. X-rays did not show what was causing all of his trouble. In exploratory surgery, Dr. Marcus Stewart discovered that all the small shoulder muscles had unraveled down into John's lower back. Some of the larger muscles had deteriorated from being detached and out of use. In seven hours of extremely delicate surgery, Dr. Stewart fastened those small muscles back to the large muscle–the rotor cuff was out of socket, so he drilled holes into the shoulder and tied the muscles together. I never cease to marvel at the miracle of modern medicine.

During the worry and painful treatment, my attitude had softened considerably. I became more tolerant of John's *extremes*, seeing them as more prankish than serious.

Because of more understanding from me, he seemed to regard me less resentfully if not as an ally. Even then, without knowing why, I had an occasional lapse into an uneasy sense of watching for some unknown threat. Waiting for the ax to fall!

It fell in the most unexpected way. Out on the town with John, a woman walked up to me and flatly, loudly announced that my husband had asked her to meet him at his apartment. I was stunned. I had not known he had an apartment. An intense pain shot through my heart. Gazing directly into my eyes, she said, "You seem like a decent person, and I think you should know this." I could see that she was telling the truth.

I thought of times when I had been suspicious, but John always managed to give a plausible excuse for names and numbers left in his pockets, and for phone calls I answered when no one seemed to be on the line. All the little snide comments and innuendoes of the past were back to haunt me.

The episode in the Western Lounge momentarily took away my will to live. I had fought this battle far too long to continue. Had it not been for Andy and Don I'm sure I would have gone over the edge. I was all that stood between them and the despair I had learned to live with; in one clear moment, I knew that my pain because of John was secondary to the pain of failing my sons. I had no choice *but to make a clearly defined choice for them.* They loved their father deeply. And he loved them.

I could no longer live in denial I had to put it to rest one way or another. No matter how elaborate John's lies were, I knew with certainty that they were lies. At first I spent my time visualizing John with other women, and berating myself *What's wrong with you, woman? I would ask myself. Have you no pride? Are you just going to go on as if nothing happened…for all you know, is happening all the time!*

My typical way of handling every problem was no longer working. All of those brighter "tomorrows" no longer held the promise I'd always counted on. Nor could I dismiss my present state of mind. The raw wounds to my heart continued to bleed.

I've often wondered what I would have done without Linda Parish. Usually outspoken, she held her counsel and mostly listened while I poured out my heart to her day after day. If it happened to be one of the days when I was angry and wanting to hit back, she agreed with me. If it was one of my calmer times of making excuses for John's ways, she quietly held her peace. By the time he left for Denver, even after that horrible summer we had drifted back to what was pretty normal for us. I did what was expected of me and John did as he pleased.

Upon arrival in Denver, John demanded more money and a two-year contract. Afraid he would never be the same after his shoulder surgery, the Broncos' front office traded him to the Miami Dolphins. Making this unexpected change was a jolt at first, but the friendliness of the players and coaching staff cushioned it for John.

It didn't take long for him to discover that Miami was a much more exciting, wide open city in which to practice his favorite "hobbies" than Denver. The boys and I had barely got settled in an apartment before John had joined the revelers and was swinging merrily along with the night crowd.

Almost every night after practice, he was out drinking. I never knew when or *if* he would be home. On rare occasions, he would come in for dinner, play with the boys, watch TV and talk normally to me. On other nights, if he came in drinking, he would throw the food I served him on the floor, plate and all. I forced myself to quietly clean up the mess without complaint, but a monster of hatred and

rebellion was building inside me. I knew from bitter experience that to cross him in any way only brought on more violence so I endured his tantrums in stoic silence. Andy and
Don knew all the signs; they fled the scene quickly if
"Daddy" came home drunk. They weathered it much better
than I not knowing what to expect kept me so nervous and
stressed out that I was utterly exhausted most of the time.

Still, I kept it from my parents. Once when John had not
been home in two days, Dad called. I was half out of my
mind at the time, but I pretended everything was fine. The
team had returned from an out-of-town game, but John
didn't come home. We had only been in Miami a short time
and I didn't know any of the players' wives well enough to
ask help with something that personal to me. I finally made
a few discreet inquiries and found out that he had made the
flight back with the team. Knowing he was somewhere in
Dade County didn't help my feelings; I really began to
worry the next day when he was still not home. I called the
hospitals, the police department, and even the State
Highway Patrol, just in case they had a report of his arrest
or injury.

With no idea where else to turn, I decided to call my
mother. Upon hearing her cheery "Hello," my courage left
me. "Hey, Mom!" I said enthusiastically; "Guess what?
I've decided to fly home early for Christmas this year.
A bunch of the wives are doing it. We aren't going to make
the playoffs anyway."

"You're what?" she interrupted; "Are the children all
right?"

"Yes, they're fine. I've just decided to bring the kids and
fly to Memphis this week."

"No, Nancy. I don't think you should do that. You need
to stay there with John. He needs you there till the season
is over. That will be best for everybody."

I couldn't see any point in burdening her now with the truth when I had gone to such lengths to cover it up for this long. My present situation would resolve itself when John finally came staggering home. Just as he always had.

I sighed, and meekly agreed with her. "You're probably right, Mom. I was just missing you and Dad."

"We miss you, too, honey. Give the boys a hug for me. It will be more fun for all of you when John can come, too."

I numbly hung up the phone. I wanted my Mama and Daddy to take care of me and make everything right again, but I couldn't tell them about the slough of despair my life had become. I felt deserted and alone. I couldn't even cry. I had already cried all my tears. I felt that even my tear ducts had dried up.

Of course John came home. Unshaven, rumpled, and smelling of stale bars. And life continued as usual.

Going home to Memphis that year was all I had thought about for weeks. The morning after we arrived, I was up and dressed before seven. I was knocking on Linda's door soon afterward. Grabbing a jacket, she said, "Let's walk."

She insists on stopping in a doughnut shop for coffee. Sitting across from each other in a booth, she says, "Okay, spill your guts. I can guess what it's been like in the fast lane. Just give me the dirt."

I laugh, and suddenly my eyes overflow. It just feels so good to be here! And I feel so safe! As if nothing can touch me. "Let's see," I said; "Do you want to hear about the time he disappeared for three days, or the night he got arrested for sleeping in the middle of the street?"

"No... that's much too tame! You can do better than that!"

"Oh, well there's always the wedding reception he interrupted in his underwear...."

Linda reached out to squeeze my hand. "I'm so, so glad you're home."

This was what I had needed. To be welcomed. Appreciated. Loved.

Without words, or philosophies, or advice, I had arrived at the apex of my dilemma. I knew with an unshakable certainty something I should have seen from the beginning. There had never been for me a choice to make. From the moment I had looked into John's eyes, it was settled. I smiled at all the times I had told myself over the years, *if it gets any worse, I'll go. If he can convince me that he no longer loves me, I'll leave. When I can't take it any more, I'm gone!*

Our song, the one that had drawn our naive, romantic notions into focus, whose lyrics had painted a parallel for our emotions, was the key which opened Pandora's box. We had chosen our destiny in that one magical moment we met, and I would make no attempt to change it. Was there, as some believed, a Great Someone who pulled the strings to direct our lives? I would have said I believed in God, but for that moment, I could not have told exactly who He was to me. But I suddenly knew without a shadow of doubt that He had in an awesome way involved Himself in my life.

~ *Chapter Eight* ~

The middle years of John's professional career remind me of a fast moving train headed for an unscheduled destination. You're never quite sure where you're going, so you can't relax and enjoy the scenery. You don't dare go to sleep because you may get put off in the middle of nowhere without a ticket for the next stop.

The experiences that stand out are never the ones you would choose to hold forever to your heart as the ones that shape your life. They are instead those painful attempts to struggle your way to the surface just to breathe the clean air again. The most consistent element in those years was John. When I thought I could see a ray of hope that he was becoming less unprincipled, he would prove me wrong. The only round in that battle that I ever won was when I balked at getting him out of jail. The night I stood my ground on that issue was nerve-wracking, but I refused to waver.

When he called to tell me to come and bail him out, I said nothing. John said, "Nancy, did you hear what I said? I said, come down here and get me out," I said, "I heard you, but I'm not coming."

For a moment, silence. Then, "Nancy, did you hear me? What do you mean you're not coming?"

And I said clearly, "I mean, I am not coming." I was a little nervous when he came home the next morning, but he didn't say a word about our conversation. I thought of the old saying, *The more things change, the more they stay the same.*

As we were preparing to return to Miami for John's third season with the Dolphins, he was traded to the Patriots. Upset at first, we soon were caught up in the excitement of change. John had always looked on being traded as rejection, which in some cases it was. When he learned that the New England team had traded Nick Buoniconti to get him, he began to see the change in a different light. I wasn't sure about leaving my southern roots behind; I wondered how well I would adjust to what I believed would be a totally different culture. Whenever anyone from up north disagreed with our relaxed, southern way of handling a situation, we casually explained it as "their Yankee attitude."

To my delight, I immediately fell in love with Boston. A beautiful city with an old-world aura about it and steeped in historical background. I could hardly wait to start exploring it. I collected landmark guides, brochures with maps and schedules in my plan for family fun. Andy and Don got excited about it, too, but we had one defector. John, in his typical way of settling things said pleasantly, "Ya'll just go right ahead without me; we can all go back together sometime. You can tell me about it."

I didn't argue. "Okay. We're going to Old North Church and learn more about Paul Revere today. If you change your mind, let us know."

I thought I had recently detected a slight change in his attitude, even when he was drinking. I'd been trying new tactics ever since we went home from Miami for the summer. I had always given in to him because he forced the issue, and I could see no choice but to knuckle under. It occurred to me that *I always have a choice in how I react.*

So I decided to respond to whatever he did by remaining calm and pleasant. I would kill him with kindness.

The one approach I hadn't tried with John was to make myself absolutely indispensable to him. I could see how much he needed me, but he ignored what I did as if I didn't exist. I wanted *him* to see me as more than an occasional convenience.

I started making a point of being there to pack what he needed for out-of-town trips, of hiding little treats among his personal effects. I was not above showing affection in ways to get his attention. If he had an especially tough game coming up, I would slip a little note of encouragement in his sock drawer, or under his plate. He didn't comment, but I felt rewarded when I would catch him looking at me with a half-smile. So... it only meant I was stupidly hoping for the impossible. Desperate people do stupid things!

Although I certainly hoped the end result would be favorable for me, it was not my intention to be devious or hypocritical. I loved John and wanted what was best for him. And I believed with all my heart that what was best for him was to be the husband and father he should be. The boys were already getting old enough to look forward to doing the things their father did. I heard them talk about helping Dad "beat up the bad guys," and going out with him to do "night stuff." I may be out of the loop, but could guess what their idea of night stuff included. Drinking and staying out all hours.

The Pats had a Sunday afternoon game in New York with the Jets, and while we were there, John actually took time to tour the city with us. We saw it all, from Central Park to the Statue of Liberty, from the subway to the top of the Empire State Building! I loved every minute of it; it was a thrill to me because we enjoyed it together as a family.

Our second trip to The Big Apple was memorable for several reasons. My sister, Janet, was getting married, so when New England played in New York the following season, she and I made plans to meet there and shop for her trousseau. What fun! We couldn't wait to hit Fifth Avenue! I reserved a room for us in the same hotel where the Patriots were staying. I couldn't stay with John; he had to room with the team.

One morning I decided to go up to his room before Janet and I went shopping. I had barely got inside his room when there was a knock on his door. John motioned for me to hide in the bathroom because I wasn't supposed to be there. No women were allowed in the players' rooms.

It was the hotel detective! He had seen me get off the elevator on that floor, and suspecting I was up to something, had followed me. "Where is she?" he asked John. It was useless for John to try to persuade him there was no one there; he had seen me enter the room.

"I know she's in here," the detective argued. "You know hookers are not allowed in this hotel!" Reaching around John, he flung open the bathroom door. Yanking me out by my arm, he started for the door pulling me along with him.

By then John was mad. "Get your hands off her," he yelled; "She's my wife!" "Oh, yeah, Buddy! I'm sure she is! Just come with me, sister; I'm taking you downstairs to security, and they'll call the cops to come get you." The detective was adamant.

I was ready to cry. "John, do something! This man really believes I'm a prostitute. He's going to have me arrested! I don't want to go to jail!"

John started pleading with him. "Hey, Mister, this isn't funny. You can't do this; she really is my wife! Just let me call one of the coaches and he'll tell you! I'm not lying to you." I guess he decided we were telling the truth when John offered to call the coach. He agreed to let John make the call, and one of the coaches came to identify me. My brief career as a hooker was over, but not before lots of jokes went the rounds. It also ended any sudden whim I had to visit John in a room reserved for players.

———»·«———

Our stay in Boston turned out to be the highlight to me of John's career. Andy, Don and I spent many happy hours together in the parks and waterfronts. Boston Commons was a special favorite. The oldest city park in the nation, it is home for many magnificent ancient trees. The kids looked forward to going there to ride the Swan Boats all around the lake.

I was drawn to the tall, narrow townhouses of Back Bay. Almost touching along cobblestone streets, they were charming reminders of the past. The reclusive mansions of Beacon Hill were elegant with their flower gardens tucked around them like a spinster's skirts.

The sight of the placid Charles River, reflecting the autumn colors of turning leaves, could leave me breathless. The bridges that span it from Boston to Cambridge left a beautiful picture that I shall always carry in my mind. I was at once captivated by Boston's elegance and comforted by its history. To me, it is a city that reaffirms America's ideals while offering a sense of continuity. When we left there, I went with a feeling of having left behind something precious and irretrievable.

Once again our homegoing to Memphis presaged a trip to Campbell Clinic for John. He was so battered he required knee and elbow surgery before he could play again. He worked hard to return to top playing form and was in excellent shape when only two weeks before camp, he was knocked off his feet by an appendectomy!

When the hospital released him, he flew immediately to Boston, though his incision was far from healed.

Disappointed that he couldn't practice with his usual intensity, he retreated into his old comfort zone: the nearest bar. Angry at the turn of events, he started fights in most of the places he frequented, which of course didn't set well with the coaches. They replaced him with another player as an example to the team, then traded him to the Green Bay Packers.

I was relieved that we had made a decision for the boys and me to stay in Memphis until we knew for certain that he would be playing the `71 season in Boston. After the Packers put him on waivers, he returned home. And I went to work trying to convince him that some other team would soon be calling him.

As if on cue, John received a call from Coach Norm Van Brocklin of the Atlanta Falcons. Over the years I had watched him pursue his *Holy Grail*: his yearning for approval from his peers. After we were married, it became clearer to me that much of his self-inflicted misery was because of his lack of a loving relationship with his father. While he lived at home with his family, he tried to earn his dad's approval. It never happened.

In San Diego for a game, we received word that John's father had died. We flew home for the funeral. This man had died without ever having once told his son that he loved him and was proud of him.

As a Falcon, on a frozen field in Minnesota, John received the injury that ended his career. The cartilage popped out of his right knee socket. By the time he got back to Atlanta, his knee was the size of his head. Every athlete knows that the surgery isn't the worst part of fixing an injury; it is the rehabilitation period where you work to regain body strength. It was a time for serious consideration of what was best for our family. When John made his decision to retire, I began dreading the aftermath.

In May of `72 when he announced his retirement, he had played seven years missing only four games. Confirming my worst fears, his wild, undisciplined ways seemed to intensify. He went back to his former job with the fire alarm company, but in his free time he was drinking, fighting and stirring things up at night. And taking his frustration out on the boys and me. Strangely, Andy and Don seemed to have steeled themselves to endure whatever came, in much the same way I did. They were only ten and eleven at the time, but they had learned enough to avoid open confrontation.

I still tried to believe that showing love and patience would eventually soften John but I had to admit to myself that there was no indication it was working. His temper just seemed to get nastier every day. At home, he was drunk and mean, and I hated the fearful, anxious way the boys and I tried to stay out of sight.

And a new fear eclipsed by far the old, momentary fear of the cruelties constantly heaped upon us. The occasional bursts of anger and a sullen moodiness in Andy or Don could plunge me into despair—a bitter despair rooted in resentment against its penalty to the innocent. *What will become of my boys?* Deep down, I knew the real question was, "What will my boys become?"

In spite of his abusive nature, John was a good provider. He had always allowed me to run the household and pay the bills. He never complained about the way I spent the money. To some, we may have appeared to be a normal family. But even as I tried to perpetuate this image, I hated the hypocrisy of our lives and blamed it all on John.

~ *Chapter Nine* ~

The pot roast is tender, the salad is crisp, and John, having graced us with his presence, seems sober as a judge. "Nancy, I have to tell you, this is a great dinner. Are these home-made rolls?"

"Made with my own two hands." *What is going on here?*

"She made chocolate pie, too, Dad." Don couldn't resist getting in on the occasion of his dad's good mood.

"That's great, Son! Maybe we'll have a scoop of ice cream on the side."

He turned to me. "Hey, Nancy, I've been thinking... I was talking to some of the guys at work today; and I was thinking it might be nice to have some of them over. We could invite the owners, the sales staff and all the wives. You used to love parties. It would give you a chance to know all of them better. Don't you think we could do that?"

John suggesting a party? Wonderful! I loved parties, though we rarely went to one because of my reluctance to deliberately choose to go where there was drinking. But I had never lost my love of being in a group of happy people having fun together.

I jumped right into the party mode and went to work gathering up what I would need: chairs, dishes, glasses, serving trays, and table linens. Nothing is too much trouble to me if it makes my guests more comfortable. I was taught the importance of gracious living in a home where friends were always welcome, and Mom often accused me of getting a double dose of her hospitality training.

Everything went off without a hitch; I was busily making the rounds to see that every guest was taken care of when I saw the wife of a company executive bearing down on me. Susan Brooks and I had become friends after John went to work for the company.

"Nancy, what can I do to help? Let me take those Cokes to the beverage table."

"Thanks, Susan. I was just thinking I could use two more hands."

She smiled and said, "I've been wanting to talk to you about something I think will interest you. I think we all sometimes need a change in the everyday routines of our lives. I've been going to a Bible study every Monday morning that has given me a new lease on life. I want to share it with everybody! Trish Fulghum is leading it, over at Karen Rodgers' home. I'd love it if you'd go with me Monday morning!"

"Oh, no, Susan, I don't think so. I appreciate it, but I don't think I can work it in." *What's to work in? The truth is, I'm standing here feeling a little offended that she would ask me. The only routine I need to change, I can figure out for myself!*

As the evening wore on, my mind kept returning to Susan and the way her face lit up when she talked about the Bible study. I admired Susan for her sincere humility and kindness. And the Bible study seemed really important to her. Maybe I should change my mind and go with her. By the time the evening ended and everyone was gone, I had halfway decided to take Susan up on her invitation. At least it would be a change from shopping and lunch out with whoever could go.

I dressed and gave myself a careful appraisal before leaving the house on Monday morning. I wanted to make a good impression on these women. Apparently this was the "in" thing to do, and I was being accepted into the current clique.

I didn't bother to take a Bible with me. I knew all about David and Goliath, Daniel in the lion's den, and Moses walking across the Red Sea on dry land; all the usual children's stories. What I had neglected to learn was that the Bible is God's personal Word to me! From the moment those women opened their Bibles to the book of Romans, they may as well have been talking Greek. I had no idea what any of it meant. When Trish explained about all those whom God foreknew and predestined, about being justified and glorified, she had me totally mystified. What did she mean, "there is none good, no, not one?"

I'd been good all my life, trying to do the right thing. I had neglected myself for the convenience of others, staying with an abusive husband for the sake of my family. I had never thought of myself as needing a Savior. I had attended church as a child, but not so regularly anymore. I couldn't remember how long I had believed in God but it must have been since I was very young, for some of my earliest memories included going to church.

As Trish taught directly from the Bible, I could see that something was wrong here. How had I missed the crucial element of the Christian faith? According to God's own word, my moral "goodness" would not satisfy His law. And repenting of sin? *What sin?* I was always careful about that. I hadn't killed anybody or been unfaithful to my marriage vows. I was not a liar or a thief.

As I listened, someone would break in from time to time to raise a point or ask a question. And I began to get the big picture. Where had I been in all those church services I had attended? What had blocked out all these things I was now hearing? *There's no excuse for this*, I thought. There is no excuse for me! Suddenly I was hungry, hungrier than I had ever been in my life! Hungry to know Jesus Christ, to really know him the way these women seemed to know him.

I went home that morning in a state of almost total confusion. The one thing I was certain of was that for the first time in my life, God had my undivided attention. I could not wait to get into the Bible and start reading it for myself. I wanted to know everything God had to say to me, and I wanted to know now. When he told me he loved me, I couldn't see the words for the tears. The more I read, the more I wanted to know, Somehow I found my way into the Sermon On The Mount, and knew I couldn't get out until I could emerge cleansed by the blood of Jesus. I had found my place of repentance.

I followed Him down the side of that mount knowing that whatever happens in my life from that moment on will have to come through the mighty hand of God. Of course I hadn't learned all I needed to know I had barely scratched the surface. But I was digging deeper every day. Whatever I did, I managed a time to get alone with the Lord and search the scriptures.

More than anything, I would want to tell "my story" of God's saving grace without getting "preachy," or attempting to control the sensibilities of others, for I know as well as anyone how little success most of our sermons have. (I guess we're all prime examples of that.) I only know that if the telling of my experiences can help one person keep the flame of hope from going out, it is worth far more than I can guess.

Hope is such a fragile thing, even in full flower. Mine was dashed so many times, often violently, but never extinguished. When we see another come through anything, we are encouraged to know the possibility to ourselves.

I dreaded weekends, and I knew the boys did, too. We never knew how ugly John's mood would be or what would throw him into a rage, so we tiptoed around, trying to counteract anything that might upset him. The only time of peace we had was when he passed out and slept several hours. Though nothing had changed in the way we lived at home, something was changing in me.

From the moment I had learned what being justified by faith meant, I had wanted nothing more than to surrender my life to the One who died for me. Knowing that Jesus who had no earthly biological father was born of woman by the will of God through the Holy Spirit, and lived the only sinless life, *knowing that he willingly died in the most cruel way for me, was overwhelming.*

I could sense his presence in an inexplicable way. He loved me. He knew me completely, and he still loved me. For now, that was enough. I felt clean. Light. As if a heavy burden had been lifted. Oh, my troubles were still with me. But I had an advocate. What an advocate!

I was able to detach myself from the hate-filled, hurtful words and acts John hurled at me. I began to see him in a different light. I realized that I was not responsible for his anger. I wanted more than anything for him to know the joy and peace that Christ brings, but I knew he wasn't ready to listen. I knew the one thing I could do for him that he could not control was to pray. I also asked three personal friends to pray for him.

Had I been able all those years before to make a spiritual commitment to our marriage, maybe our lives would have been different, who can say? Regrettably, at that time I had no more interest in the purposes of God than John. I'm not even clear about my reasons for staying with him. Maybe it was a selfish, possessiveness that kept me holding on. I suppose a case could be made for calling it an identity crisis. He commanded attention. In the beginning of our relationship, without realizing what I was doing, I think I was letting him define who I was. I was John's; anything else and I would lose my identity.

I had hidden the truth of our dysfunctional family as much as possible from everyone except Linda. She knew our real condition better than anyone, and gave me all the support she could. I'm so grateful for that friendship that was always there with just the response I needed in those troubling times.

As I looked back over my life from my changed perspective, I saw how I had buried reality in ways that were not only wrong, but destructive. One of the ways I struck out at John was in compulsive shopping. Spending money was my way of getting revenge for his bad behavior.

I am ashamed to remember the extremities to which I carried this vice. Not content to do it alone, I enlisted Linda in it as soon as possible after returning home to stay. I was literally obsessed with shopping! I'd go out on a whim and buy a roomful of furniture, or accessories to redecorate the whole house. And clothes; there was always a new style dress to buy. I don't know how reluctantly Linda followed my lead in those days, but we were both impulsive so she enthusiastically joined in.

After joining the Bible study group, my life changed so drastically that I lost all interest in former pursuits. Almost immediately after that first day, the idea of wandering around from mall to mall was boring to me. I was sharing my excitement with Linda and she was happy for me. She decided to join the study group, which made it even better. Now we could study together. It helped us to learn and grow much faster in spiritual truth.

Before I met Jesus face to face, there were times when I became so emotionally drained that I couldn't cope with the situation any longer. When that happened and I threatened to leave, John always sent roses and stayed home a day or two, telling me how sorry he was for what he did.

After lots of kissing, love-making and sweet together-ness, he considered everything fixed and was off with renewed energy on his never-ending round of drinking, fighting and scaring his family half to death! And I would repeat my round of excuses for him. In those days a cynical observer could have said that we celebrated the shortest honeymoons on record. And more of them.

If my life had changed, John's had not. Holding his job was not a problem because entertaining business associ-ates was an integral part of it. Guests were wined and dined at company expense. John loved it. And for obvious reasons, I hated it.

There was one very important change in John. The weeks since he had taken his anger and frustration out on me physically were stretching into months. True, I was being very diplomatic and careful to avoid any hint of chal-lenging him, but in the occasional times when he was com-pletely sober, I would look up from my studies to see him watching me. My new found "religion," seemed to confuse him. He didn't know quite what to make of this new me. Well, that made two of us. I was day by day losing my fear of what he could do to me, but I was very concerned about his effect on Andy and Don.

As I learned more about God's word and His promises, my faith grew. When I read, *For with God nothing shall be impossible, (Luke 1:37)* my confidence soared right through the ceiling. I claimed that verse as my assurance that He could save John whether *John* wanted to be saved or not. I believed it so strongly that I started trying to help God do it. I started by telling him about the joy in my heart, but he cut me off with the remark that he wanted nothing to do with what he called "religion." I tried to explain that I didn't have "religion."

"It's a personal relationship, John, a relationship with Jesus." I could have been discussing a moon landing; he had no idea what I was talking about. I had no choice but to back off and try to let him see the Spirit of Christ in my actions.

Our house was only a half-mile from Mom and Dad's. It was good to have them close, but I was more than a little concerned that they would one day run into the real John. My parents lived active, busy lives themselves, so hiding the truth from them turned out to be easier than I had thought. John was always on his best behavior when they were going to be around; he admired them and very much wanted their good opinion of him. He had worked for my father from time to time when we were at home in the off season, and was always very careful not to let Dad see the man our sons and I had to live with day to day. The boys loved staying over with their grandparents, and I was only too happy to know they were there. I always coached them not to say anything about "Daddy's drinking, or temper fits." I wanted them to love him. I guess I thought it would help us in some way.

With even the little they could not help seeing, I've often marveled at my skills as an actress. I could have challenged Sara Bernhardt with my happy act.

~ *Chapter Ten* ~

John's plane from Augusta was due in at five-thirty. I looked at the clock for what was possibly the forty-ninth time, and called the airport. *Yes, that flight landed on schedule.* That was over five hours ago. So at least he was somewhere in Memphis. As I packed his bag earlier in the week for one of his work-related seminars, I included his golf clothes. Several of the men from the company went along just for the golf games afterward. I was hoping he would join them instead of roaming the bars. The lateness of the hour told me otherwise.

He staggered in around midnight, so drunk he could hardly walk. When he lurched into the bedroom and fell across the bed, he immediately passed out and I didn't try to move him or get him undressed. Instead, I stood there crying, and praying that God would save him before he killed himself drinking.

Sometime in the hours before dawn, I had an idea. The more I thought of it, the better I liked it. I wouldn't actually have to confront him, and I would still be making a statement. In the biggest letters I could fit in across the wide vanity minor, using the brightest red lipstick I could find, I wrote: GOD IS GOING TO GET YOU! It would be the first thing he'd see when he stumbled into the bathroom nursing a hangover.

Just for good measure, I scribbled another note to him and put it in his athletic bag which was always packed and ready. He worked out at the Club several times a week, so I knew he'd take it with him when he left for work.

I pretended to be asleep when he left the next morning, but I had a chance to take a peek at him when he grabbed his duffel bag to leave. He had his mad face on. I knew by the set of his jaw and a twitching muscle that I was better off asleep. *Oh, he has seen it and he's furious! Just wait till he opens that gym bag! That note, similar to the first, said: "Jesus loves you, but he is still going to get you!"*

As it got later and later that night and he still hadn't come home, I decided to write another note. I took the boys with me in my car, and began making the rounds of John's favorite haunts. By the time I found the right one the boys were sound asleep. When I saw his car in the parking lot of one of his hangouts I stopped, and after looking around to see if anyone was watching, I opened the door and slid out. Thankfully, his car was unlocked. I had my note and sticking tape in my hand. Quickly, I taped my note to the steering wheel where he couldn't possibly miss it, no matter how drunk he was. I had written in big, bold letters: JESUS LOVES YOU, BUT HE IS DEFINITELY GOING TO GET YOU!

I knew he saw my notes. I'm sure he was waiting for me to mention them because I sometimes caught him watching me like a cat teasing a mouse. But he never said a word about them. And neither did I.

The boys and I had begun attending church with Linda's family, and when the church planned a revival, Linda and I started plotting a way to get John to go with us. We were not overly ambitious, just one night would be a step in the right direction. We carried out the plan perfectly. John knew the Parishes were members of the church, so he didn't suspect a thing when she came over and invited us to go with them one night.

As soon as she left, I played out my part. I turned on all the charm I could and begged him to take us *just one night.*

I carefully orchestrated it so he could take credit for getting us there. To my surprised delight, he agreed to go.

It was several days later that I remembered the big bouquet of red roses on the dining table that evening. I don't remember the offense that preceded the roses, but whatever it was, I thanked the Lord for finding a way to use it to my advantage.

Our night out to church together did not have the desired effect. Or maybe it did. I have learned that when we try to run ahead of God in His business, we usually get disappointed. Timing is more important than time, and God works outside all the limitations that we attempt to prescribe.

A few weeks after the revival, we had a visit from two men in the church. I answered the doorbell to find Ron Young and Ken Meador standing on our threshold. I knew they were deacons in their church. *Uh-oh!* I shook their hands in greeting, and cordially invited them into the living room, speaking loudly in hopes that John would take the opportunity to get rid of the tall beer in his hand. Ushering them in, I could see that he was empty-handed. He pleasantly offered them chairs, and I nervously sat down on the sofa next to John. He seemed a little uncomfortable at first, but as they asked a few questions about his adjustment from a professional football career to retirement and nine to five living, he loosened up.

Suddenly, Ken said, "John, are you a Christian?"

John looked back at him silently for a long moment. "Uh..." he finally said; "I've been b'ptized."

I let my breath out nervously. People just did not ask John Bramlett anything that might embarrass or anger him. Neither Ken nor Ron pursued the question further. Instead they talked for a few minutes about the difference Jesus had made in their lives. They spoke briefly of the peace and purpose he had given them by his presence within them. When they rose to go, John was gracious. Polite. Ron asked John, "Would you give up one of your sons for the sins of the World?" John said, "No! I love them too much." Ron replied, "God did that for you." At the door, Ron, who had been rather quiet, turned and looked directly at John. "Do you know why we're here, John? Do you know why we came?" "Not really. Why did you?" "We just had one reason, John. We love you."

Ron's eyes were still on John's, and John couldn't seem to look away. I could see the shock on his face. I'm sure he had never had a man tell him he loved him.

A thunderstorm had developed during Ron and Ken's visit, and at that moment, a deafening clap of thunder shook the house. I had an eerie feeling that the very voice of God was speaking directly to us. A bolt of lightening split the sky and struck nearby as we stood in the doorway watching.

I shivered, thinking, *Surely you know God is speaking to you, John. Please listen to Him before it's too late!*

While John told the men goodbye, I hurried into the bedroom and called Linda. I wanted her to be praying. I quickly told her about John's reaction to our visitors. "He didn't throw them out. He actually listened to what they said. Keep praying. I know God was in this." I hung up, and went to the living room. John wasn't there.

I started toward the kitchen, but stopped in amazement in the doorway. John was standing at the sink, pouring beer down the drain. As I watched him empty all the cans from the refrigerator, I felt the warmth of tears running down my face. He went to the liquor cabinet and began to empty the bottles into the sink. Then he sacked them all up and took them outside to the trash can. I had no idea what it all meant, but I could see he was in no mood to talk.

My mind had gone blank I wanted to let him know I was there for him, but knew somehow that anything I did would be an intrusion in something I didn't understand.

I knew he knew I was there. He seemed not to care. Brushing past me, he sat down in a chair, leaned his head back and closed his eyes. Hurt by his silence, I slipped into the bedroom and called Linda again. Whispering, I told her what he was doing, and asked, "What in the world do you think is going on?"

You don't know?" It's what we've been praying for! He is under conviction! God is doing what we have all been praying for!"

I couldn't hear a sound from the living room, so I went down the hall and looked in; John was still sitting where I had left him, but he was reading my Bible. A long time afterward, he came to bed, but when I awoke to daylight, he had already left for his office. My Bible was gone, too.

I called Linda as soon as I got the boys off to school. We must have talked for an hour. We came to the prayerful conclusion that John was searching for answers to questions which he had never before thought of asking. Questions like why are we here? What is our purpose in the scheme of things? Knowing John, especially the one about whether God is real, or wants contact with us personally. I prayed all day that he would see the grace and mercy of God, and experience His forgiveness and love.

When he came home that evening, he was very quiet and polite, but distant. He still wasn't talking, so I went on with my usual after-dinner chores. The boys and I went to bed at our usual time, leaving John sitting in the living room reading the Bible.

The next night I let the boys sleep over at Mother and Dad's. I was hoping he would talk to me if we were alone.

I think he uttered four words the entire evening. He asked, "Where are the boys?"

As soon as he ate, he opened the Bible and started reading. I was both happy and sad. Happy that he found God's Word so interesting, but feeling lonely and shut out. *After all the prayers and wonderful truths I had tried to share with him, now he is locking me out of what is happening in his heart. It isn't fair...*

Suddenly, I was feeling so ashamed. This was what I had been praying for now that it appeared to be happening, I was acting like a spoiled child. I asked the Lord to forgive me. But I forgot to ask Him to control my mouth, so I kept trying to draw John into conversation until he finally closed the Bible and went to bed.

Lying there beside him, I again felt resentment building. All the spiritual maturity I thought I had gained seemed to have escaped and flown south. Again the Holy Spirit spoke in my heart, and I knew it was up to me to take control of my attitude. That freedom of choice God gives had begun to weigh heavier and heavier. I could see but one choice for me: to stop complaining, and get my own house in order. I thought of Jacob's struggle with the angel (Gen. 32:24-32) and knew that if I, too, received God's blessing, I would get it only in and by overcoming my personal unworthy instincts.

When I finally slept, it was in the peace of having fitted myself into the proper equation with others in God's plan. I could pray for them, I could be a witness of God's grace to them, but I could neither claim credit nor take glory.

When John left for work, the turmoil in his soul was showing in his face. His miserable, haunted look broke my heart, but I was beginning to understand that this was a struggle I could not help him resolve. I gave him a quick kiss on the cheek that he hardly noticed, and brightly wished him a good day. He mumbled something unintelligible in return, and drove away. And I went back to my prayers.

This was the third day since Ron and Ken had paid him the night visit. As I thought about John's behavior in those three days, I realized he had become a stranger in our house. A stranger with amnesia off in a world of his own where no one was welcome.

By mid-afternoon, I could no longer bear the suspense of what was happening with him, so I called his office. When I asked for John, his secretary said he left instructions not to be disturbed, no matter who called.

"But I'm his wife," I said. "Surely that doesn't apply to family."

"I'm sorry, Mrs. Bramlett," she said adamantly, "But he said he didn't want to speak with anyone."

"Why isn't he accepting calls?"

"Well, I think he was reading the Bible."

That's all he had done for three days. I didn't know whether to be concerned or hopeful. I tried to explain my concern to her, and told her I was coming to the office. She seemed relieved, though I could tell she hadn't a clue as to what was going on.

When I got to his office, before I even had time to knock on his door, he flung it open and grabbed me in a bear hug. "Nancy, I just got saved! Right here in my office. Right here, down on my knees by my desk." He looked so relaxed and happy, I couldn't stop staring at him. I threw my arms around him while we laughed and cried together.

At that moment it would have been difficult to tell by looking, who was experiencing that first rush of joy that comes with the changed, new life! But for John, I have to say, his faith from the first moment, never wavered. My commitment grew more slowly. But it was enough, on that warm May evening, just to be a part of this mighty work of God in a human heart.

When we got home and told Andy and Don, they joined in the celebration. They could not have guessed on that first evening, the kind of change that was about to happen in their lives. In all our lives. John and I were on the phone immediately, trying to tell the good news to all who had so faithfully supported us with their prayers.

After the boys finally got so tired they went to bed, John and I sat at the kitchen table with a Bible between us and talked about our future a future with our lives joined together in a way we had never known: *Spiritually as well as physically!* It was an awesome evening.

~ *Chapter Eleven* ~

"Honey! Wake up! Wake up, Nancy! That's my girl!"

"Um'm." I was wide awake, *but if this is a dream, don't ever let me wake up!* I rolled over. *Who was this man wearing little other than the biggest, widest, sweetest grin I'd ever seen?*

"Honey," he said, "I just thought of someone I need to talk to I've got to tell Vic about what happened yesterday." Vic Scott was a former baseball buddy; one who had been in and out of trouble with John on many of his wild escapades.

"It can wait," I said, dragging him down for a good-morning kiss; "A few hundred years from now, maybe I'll give you time to do that."

Oh, this was rich! And it was all mine! Thank you, God! Thank you Jesus! Since that twenty-fifth day of May in 1973, I've never stopped experiencing a quick sense of wholeness every time I think of it. I had clung to our marriage in some unreasoning, inexplicable way even while I couldn't see any help in sight. Every time I was in almost total despair, something always happened to delay my giving up. I guess it was my independent nature. Sometimes, right on the brink, *something* would tell me *it's too soon to quit!* And look what happened! Stretching my arms over my head, I couldn't take the smile off my face.

Lying there in a state of complete happiness, the thought came to me that maybe we had died and gone to heaven without being aware of it! "Do you think that's possible, John?" I asked.

"No," he answered, "I just think God has given me another chance. I'm so glad He didn't just make me better than I was. If He had done that, and stopped there, it wouldn't have done any good. It took the works for me, I mean the Potter had to break that sorry old pot that wouldn't hold water, and start over. He knew it was going to take a brand new creation. I know now why Jesus said *you have to be born again! That's what happens.* I don't even think about the same things."

We couldn't stop talking. John went to work, but not before he got the boys up and hugged them, and talked to them. He was full of plans for all of us. To get into a Bible Study group. To find a church where we could all be part of a team. To begin telling our friends and our neighbors about Jesus. I was amazed. Here I was, the seasoned Christian, and overnight, he was away out in front, leading the way! *How long can this last,* I thought, and hated myself for thinking it.

I decided not to tell anyone else about John's conversion until I was certain it was genuine. While I waited, I was praying continuously for God to reveal the truth to me. I didn't have long to wait.

As hard as he had lived all out for Satan, he now lived for Christ. The attitudes and actions of his former life were completely reversed. Everywhere he went, he told everyone in his path about the difference the Lord had made in his life. Because of the phenomenal change in him, I was constantly being asked about him. To be honest, I was having some trouble handling John's salvation. I was a little embarrassed by his public witness. As I would stand by waiting while he talked to the man carrying out groceries, or pumping gas, I'd think, *Lord, I wanted him to be saved, but is this really necessary?*

As we had expected it would, John's status at work changed immediately. In no other setting was his changed personality more clearly seen or keenly felt. The love of partying, boozing, and fighting had gone out of him, and that wasn't unanimously viewed as an improvement by the fire alarms systems company. He tried to continue with his selling, but he didn't `fit in with the guys' anymore. At out-of-town seminars, he couldn't resist witnessing to the bellhops, the maids, the waiters, management anyone he could collar. I could see how that wouldn't set well with company officials who are paying an excellent salary to have their product promoted. John knew he was on shaky ground; he was just following the prompting of the Spirit within him.

Sensing John's discomfort with the situation, I questioned whether or not he should continue to work in that atmosphere. The great change we had experienced suggested to us that John needed to make a career change; one that would give him more opportunities to be as evangelistic as he liked. So, after much discussion and prayer, he quit his job. It didn't enter our minds that finding a new job would be difficult. We assumed that the Lord had a place waiting that would provide us with the comfortable lifestyle to which we had become accustomed. Had we known what lay ahead, I wonder if we would have had the courage for John to leave that profitable position.

It was five months before he found another position. During that time, he left the house every day, just as if he had a job. He stayed busy witnessing to people everywhere he went. When he found someone down on his luck, he became an instantaneous benefactor. I never knew who was coming to dinner. If he found a hitchhiker needing a change of clothes, he brought him home to clean him up. I was having a hard time making ends meet. With no money coming in I was skimping and saving all I could, but it was getting harder and harder to buy groceries with my limited means. We were rapidly using up what we had saved over the years.

When I expressed my worries about money, I could count on a big smile from John, and the reassurance that God would provide. When I was concerned for his safety, I was more insistent: "John, you have got to stop picking up hitchhikers. It's crazy! You could be killed! Don't you watch the news? People who stop to help strangers are being robbed, having their car stolen, or worse. Please stop it, John I'm worried about you!"

He would hug me and cheerfully offer me another strong dose of positive faith. And tell me that he was just trying to do for others what those two men who loved him did for him. When I realized that nothing was going to make him stop reaching out to strangers, I was forced to trust God to take care of him.

"I've never seen such a saved man," I complained to Linda. "He never lets up! And get this: Do you think he ever asks *me* anything about the Bible? Of course not. He understands it better than I do."

"Well, for goodness sake, Nancy, what did you expect? He's a man, isn't he? Did you think he was going to let *you* teach *him*?"

As I stood there looking at her, she said, "Oh, come on, Nancy, are you listening to yourself? There's no such thing as being over-saved! Which had you rather have, the old John Bramlett or the new one? He's on fire for the Lord, Nancy! You need to just get in there and help him."

I knew she was right. From the moment God saved John, he had given him the great spiritual gift of evangelism. I realized that, and as I saw the longing in him to share with others what he had been given, I began praying fervently to receive that nurturing spirit for myself

I learned a very valuable lesson in those times of physical insecurity. John was right. Where I could see only darkness or a blank wall, I was constantly encouraged by the Spirit of the Savior within me. The deeper the need, the greater my urgency to hold on to Jesus. I must have read His prayerful words for believers in the book of John at least a hundred times in those troubling days. As I clung to my faith, I was receiving little nudges moving me forward; instances of favor from unexpected sources. And I was beginning to actually see the literal hand of God in my life. Just as it's always there, in every life.

As word spread about John's new life, he began receiving invitations to speak in churches, civic organizations, and in chapel services of colleges and schools in the area. When they responded to him with "love offerings," he was too proud to take money for his services. The pastor in one of the churches took John aside and gently led him to see that to refuse a love offering would deprive people of fulfilling their responsibility to support the Lord's work.

"They deserve to know the joy of giving," he said. "John, it's Biblical. Read First Timothy 5:18: 'The laborer is worthy of his reward.'

Some of his first out-of-state speaking engagements were to professional teams for whom he had played during his career. I think he enjoyed those most of all because he knew they could see what Jesus had done for him.

Employment came when John formed a company with another man who sold air filters to industrial plants. Profits were minimal, and the man soon wanted out, leaving us with unpaid product bills. We had no choice but to somehow make it work. The boys and I pitched in, and John struck a deal with Ron Young to buy parts at a discount. Even that was not enough to offset the debt we had inherited. In spite of our best efforts, Bramlett Industrial Supply Company failed miserably.

John was a good salesman. What he was not was a good collector. He was too kindhearted to push people to pay. By the time we realized we could not collect enough to keep our heads above water, we had run up a huge debt on Ron Young's books.

Mr. Young graciously gave John a job and took a portion of his salary each week until the debt was paid. It took ten years. During that time, I tried to think of ways to help out financially.

Not willing to give up my determination to help, I went to my usual, impulsive accomplice: Linda. Whenever one of us needed something from the other, we always ended up saying, "Count me in," regardless of how we felt about it. Meeting the need was the important issue. We pledged our support, then discussed our reservations. That way, we were always there for each other. With money tight, we dived into several selling ventures at once, peddling everything from make-up to macrame, to home sewing.

None of it ever amounted to much, but it made me feel that I was contributing. And I needed that.

Christmas was coming, and knowing our circumstances, I began to panic. We had always spent so lavishly on gifts, and I worried about what I could do. By then, I should have known better. One Sunday morning, sitting quietly in church listening to the choir singing, *Joy To The World*, my heart was filled with such joy that I could hardly sit still. I could feel the presence of Christ as the words of that beautiful song proclaimed: *The Lord Is Come—Let Earth Receive Her King!* I felt so ashamed of my worries as I realized we had been given that good news of great joy to all people: that babe in the manger who is Christ, the Lord!

Our first Christmas with Him was our best ever! As the true significance of why we celebrate filled my heart, I began to pray that God would teach me to trust Him. I could see that I had a long way to go. I wanted to learn, as the Apostle Paul had, how to be content with whatever was God's will for me, knowing that He knew best. I wanted to grow spiritually to the place of trusting when my eyes were incapable of seeing His purposes. To always thank Him and praise Him, no matter what!

~ Chapter Twelve ~

Lord, you know they're in my heart, and I know they're in yours, but how do we get YOU into theirs?

The realization that I was holding in my hands the key to the literal kingdom of God was so overpowering to me that I began to pray for my children as I had prayed for John. I was so grateful that we had seen the light while they were still in their impressionable years. Still teachable. When I came across something I thought would speak to them, I began sharing portions of the Bible with them. At the same time, it was developing in me a method of study. Whatever the subject, they always had questions that I knew they expected me to answer. Consequently, when I read Scripture, I attempted to analyze word by word, its deeper meaning.

I first became aware that it was producing fruit when both Andy and Don joined the church with us. John and I had explained as clearly as we could how to commit our lives to Jesus, and both boys were eager to be a part of it. I've come to understand in recent years that in Christ, nothing is ever permanently settled except eternal destination. A few years after his "conversion," Andy came home from a church camp to tell us that while there, he had a real experience with the Lord.

"I know you thought I was okay," he said. "I really wasn't. I hadn't changed inside. Well, I don't know how to explain it to you, but now I know the difference. I know I'm okay."

Afterward, John and I discussed it. We had learned something new. Everything is current in God's sight. It had been so clearly illustrated to us through Andy. When he had gone forward in church to become a follower of Christ with us, he was committing to the fringe benefits: the sweetness of peace and joy in his home.

God had blessed Andy's commitment and had watched over him until he placed him in that church camp to hear a witness speak of a relationship that he knew he didn't have — a relationship he wanted.

In every simple experience, I was seeing more and more the amazing ways of God's grace. Hearing Pastor Adrian Rogers of Bellevue Baptist Church explain the wonders of grace, I could imagine no higher calling than for a human soul to awaken to its sufficiency.

Dr. Rogers used a river as an analogy of God's grace. As the river's waters flow past, they are passing from our sight to be replaced by the continuing stream of more waters. The current that takes them forward is now flowing before us with different water, although it is the same river. So flows God's grace toward us.

As God permits me to learn, the grace I experience from Him is mine to pass on to those who hunger for it. As currents of His grace, we have no choice but to open the floodgates that allow grace upon grace to flow into the lives of others.

Little did I realize the impact of the headwaters of the Source of grace. As I struggled to fit what I could do into a place of service, I could not have guessed what the Lord had in mind. Speaking publicly of private matters was not something I could envision myself doing. When I was invited to share my personal experiences with a group of young mothers at First Assembly of God on Highland Avenue, I was petrified. But I had promised the Lord to go where He led, so I went. I told Him I was willing, but if He wanted me to stand up in front of a roomful of people and speak, He had better do something to keep my knees from buckling.

As I gave my testimony to those gracious young women, my insecurities melted away. I should have known, the God we serve is well able to equip us with whatever we need to honor His call. That first speaking engagement led to several more invitations in the Memphis area and in the Mid-South. I responded with the conviction that this was the Lord's special purpose for me.

As more and more of our time was caught up in ministering, circumstances far outside our control seemed to be pulling us toward a concerted, full-time ministry. John was booked up for so many places ahead that it became apparent to us that we needed to find some way of resolving our two worlds into one entity. Unknown to us, E. W. Atkinson and his brother, George, had become interested in John's work with people. After George's death later that year, E. W. proposed to John that they begin The John Bramlett Ministry in honor of George.

At his own expense, E. W. had his attorney draw up a charter and register it with the state. When the charter was granted, the John Bramlett Ministries, Inc. was born, but it would be seven years before we would go into ministry full time. Business men around the city who knew the sacrifices John was making in order to witness, pitched in to help by giving money to buy gas, tracts, and Bibles.

In 1985, when our debt to Ron Young was paid in full, John resigned his job in order to work in ministering full time. Not only did the Lord increase opportunities to serve, but He also provided the resources. In times of need, help would came from such unexpected sources that we often marveled at God's ways of blessing. We were humbled by the obvious recognition that God's gifts to us were being poured out for his purposes. Certain scriptures took on new meaning to us. "For it is God which worketh in you, both to will and to do of His good pleasure." (Phil.2:13) He not only urges us forward by his Word, but he shares His joy with us as we are obedient to his direction. We may not understand why things are happening as they are. It took me a while to learn that understanding can wait obedience cannot!

Paul and Judy Kuhlman are a perfect example of God's sovereign will at work bringing people together for His purposes, proving "His hand is not shortened, that it cannot save, neither his ear heavy, that it cannot hear." (Isa.59: I) We moved around the corner from the Kuhlmans not long after we were saved. Our children were in school together, so we knew them casually. We didn't know that their marriage was in trouble because of Paul's drinking and workaholic lifestyle.

With just a fence between our back yards, every time John heard a sound from them, he was over that fence and talking to Paul about the joy of knowing the Lord! As Judy and I became closer friends, she began sharing her doubts about staying in her marriage. And I was assuring her that giving up on it was not the answer Jesus Christ was! As we talked at length about the difference the Lord could make, she told me that she had believed in Him when she was a child, but had never made Him a part of her life. She supported the principles Christ exemplified and taught; she had just never had a personal relationship with Him.

Encouraged by my enjoyment in studying the Bible, she decided to become involved in Bible Study Fellowship. I was blessed to be a group leader for many years with Jonetta Fargarson, my teaching leader. Those years in Bible Study Fellowship laid the foundation in my personal growth as a Christian woman. She, like myself in earlier years, found new strength and hope in its disciplines. We continued to pray for Paul, and one morning we heard a knock on the door that brought all four of us into a celebration that continues today in our hearts. Paul had experienced the miracle of being reborn into the kingdom of God.

———»•«———

Our sons, Andy and Don, spent their teenage years in an atmosphere so different to the one they knew as young children. Happily married now with homes of their own, I often reflect on the miracle of grace that gave them passage out of the miserable way we once lived.

Throughout the years since we committed our future to the Lord's use, we have been overwhelmed by the goodness of Christian friends. One friend of the ministry offered to build us a home at his cost. Our old home was bursting at the seams, and he thought we needed more space for all the house guests we welcomed over the course of a year's activities.

While the new home was under construction, John was invited to Ft. Myers Beach, Florida, to preach in a revival. Our friends, Bob and Mary Katherine Burch invited me to come along with John and make a vacation of it. It was a wonderful time of fellowship with this pastor and wife that we had met at a Bible Conference. We were returning to their house from the Sunday evening service when I received a phone call from my sister, Janet. Dad had suffered a major heart attack that afternoon. Though Janet assured me that he was stable, something in me that had never before been touched warned that my life was never going to be the same again.

~ Chapter Thirteen ~

A sense of urgency possesses me. I must go! My daddy is waiting! He can't leave without me! Wait! Don't go! I won't let you go!

Tears are streaming down my face, and my pillow is wet. I must have made a sound, for immediately, John's arms are around me and I am sobbing into his chest. Sh-h-h! It's all right. You're okay. Everything's all right, Honey Sh-h-h.

Everything is not all right! Nothing will ever be all right again. My daddy's gone and I'm never going to be anybody's little girl again!

After Janet's phone call to Florida, my spirit was so disturbed that my inner turmoil seemed like the only reality. All I could think of was that I must get home quickly what if my father died before I could reach him?

John was frantically calling all the airlines, but no one had a flight before morning. We had no choice but to make a reservation for the first flight out, and go to bed. I didn't dare close my eyes; my entire being was focused on praying for my father's life to be spared. *Just let me get there, God Please, just let me see him smile at me one more time, Lord! Help me! Please help me!*

The flight from Florida to Memphis seemed interminable, but at last we were there, speeding toward Baptist Central Hospital. Linda Parish and Pat Brand had greeted us at our gate. Dad was alive, but very weak. Pat, a registered nurse and Linda, a medical assistant, tried to prepare me for how my father would look, hooked up to all the life support systems. Nothing could have prepared me.

He was so frail and helpless, so pale and weak. When I walked into the room, I had one quick thought of being a strong witness of the peace and power of God. Then I collapsed into convulsive sobs.

Very thankful to find him alive, I couldn't leave his side. The next few days all ran together for me, converging into one long, extended prayer that he would come through this, and live.

By the middle of the week, he was showing signs of improvement. He seemed stronger, and had a revived interest in what went on around him. On Thursday, he watched a golf tournament, and I was sure he was going to recover his old vitality. His doctor cautiously restricted his speaking, but allowed him to scribble notes to us for what he wanted. His notes mostly said, "Go home," and we could never figure out if he meant for us to go home, or if he wanted to go home. Or if he had a sense somehow, that he was going home to heaven. We never knew.

On Sunday following the Sunday he suffered the attack, my precious father went home to His Lord. I don't think my mother had left the hospital from the day he entered. Janet and I knew we had to make the funeral arrangements, and try to get through this awful, unspeakable loss. In the death of someone so near and dear, I learned that God places a defense mechanism in us that shields us from the sudden hopelessness that threatens to swallow us up. I don't know how people bear the unbearable without a loving God to sustain them.

While friends came and went, offering their sympathy and support, I went through the motions of what I had to do, in a state of numbness. This seems to be the way God's "defense mechanism" works to hold us together until we can receive enough of His grace to see our loss as He sees it. At first, my self-pitying grief prevented God's healing

Spirit from reaching me. We are sometimes the greatest barrier to receiving the healing we so desperately need.

Actually, as I listened to the great numbers of people, many I didn't even know, tell what Warren Andrews had meant to them, I was beginning to heal. My mind was filled with gratitude to have had this exemplary man for my earthly father. As the Lord filled my mind, day to day with beautiful memories, I began to get a clearer picture of what it means to die in Christ. *Of what it means to live in Christ!* In the intensity of my grief, I tried to cling to the triumph of what my dad must be experiencing in those first moments of heaven. He was at home with the Savior he loved.

My Mama `Lotta was a pillar of strength during those days. She never once asked why she had lived to give up a child to the grave. And it occurred to me that she must be seeing it from God's point of view. He gave His son for us, and Mama 'Lotta felt that she could do no less than graciously allow her son to reap the joys Jesus had died to give him. In fact, I began to get an entirely new perspective toward death.

As soon as I began to take control of my mournful thoughts and ask God to mold them to his will, I knew I was on the right track. God spoke in my heart, in the still, small voice I had learned to depend upon. "Nancy, your dad is well now, and alive forever more. Would you have wanted him to stay with you, unable to enjoy the life he loved? It is in love and mercy that I called him home." I felt God's nearness in that moment, and because of that I was able to celebrate in my heart the great gift of Dad's life. I know today that to refuse God's sovereign will in this is a denial of the blessing our loved ones are to us. Death brings sorrow, but the contribution of their lives with us is worthy of celebration.

My mother's healing was slow and painful, but she, too, realized the great gift we all received through the love of this wonderful man. Janet's family, my own, and a great host of friends all drew closer in a spirit of thanksgiving for a life well-lived.

Two years later, Mama `Lotta was gone. I had given a surprise birthday party for her in our new home and we all marveled at her wit and humor. At ninety, she was still driving her car, doing her own shopping , and keeping up the normal activities she had done for years.A fall broke her hip and she never recovered. There had been a time when I would have had difficulty accepting her death, but I knew she was ready, even anxious, to go. There is no feeling that compares to the confidence we feel when those we love, love the Lord. In the face of death, we can trust God to bring us safely home.

~ *Chapter Fourteen* ~

Yes! Yes! Yes!

I was standing at the kitchen sink, thinking of how I was going to squeeze a large number of young mothers into our living room for a group Bible Study. Mentally rearranging furniture, opening up areas to expand space, I would allow nothing to hinder my goal in launching my dream. Since the first day of our life with Jesus became a reality, John and I had concentrated on ways to share the good news with others.

Our goal was always to minister, but initially, John practiced it far more successfully than I. I now see that this was because I had not understood the real nature of ministry. I finally realized I was doing it without knowing it! And that beautiful "Y" word, *Yes*, became my marching order.

It took a godly older Christian to point out to me that I was not only involved in ministering, but *I had a ministry!* To suddenly realize that my dreams of bringing relief to hurting women could bear fruit, was an inspiring revelation to me. I was ready to face Satan down with no more than a prayer and a promise! We can never underestimate the power of the prayer, but it is the promise that gives us the courage.

As my studies became more purposeful, I was constantly amazed at the wealth of meaningful promises I had either overlooked or dismissed as not applicable to me. I was suddenly inundated with promises. John 15:7: "If ye abide in me, and my words abide in you, ye shall ask what ye will, and it shall be done unto you."

Psalm 126:6: "He that goeth forth and weepeth, bearing precious seed, shall doubtless come again with rejoicing, bringing his sheaves with him."

Isaiah 30:21: "And thine ears shall hear a word behind thee, saying This is the way, walk ye in it, when ye turn to the right hand, and when ye turn to the left."

My life verse became Phil 4:13, "I can do all things through Christ, who strengthens me.

I was no longer content to use only one avenue of serving, to reach people. I felt that through practice I had gained confidence in speaking to groups, but I now had a vision of what could be done through each one, individually. I was seeing the wasted talent in all of those who have never looked within themselves to see the spiritual gift God so generously gave them. And I was on fire to resurrect it!

Since that day, my ministry has been to young women in particular, primarily because I can never forget the silent suffering of those early years of marriage to an abusive husband. In testimony, I always hasten to point out the difference the light of Jesus can make, even when it only exists within the victim. When the Holy Spirit came to live within me, although for a brief time the verbal abuse became more incessant, the burden was easier to bear, for I was not alone.

When prayers were answered bringing John to Jesus, he became overnight, the husband and father that is every woman's dream. Wrongs were set right. Where once my heart had bled for myself and our sons, all my compassion became centered on John's regret for past sins. When I looked into his eyes, I could see the suffering there. He knew he was forgiven, but it was a very long time before he was able to forgive himself

As I look back on my background of suffering through stressful situations, I can see how God used those times to create in me a sensitivity to the needs of women today. Women with small children are particularly vulnerable to the temptation to give up to throw up their hands and say, "Okay, I quit!" I realize how near I came to that decision many times, but something, *Someone* always held me.

I believe my endurance was no less than the ultimate will of God in placing me where I am today. Who can say how many are called for a moment in time, called for a purpose they may never know? Like the message from Mordecai to Queen Esther, "Who knoweth whether thou art come to the kingdom for such a time as this?" (Esther 4:14) Standing there in my kitchen praying for all the young mothers who could benefit from the kind of ministry I had in mind, I realized that my house would not hold them.

Our membership in a church as large as Bellevue meant that the potential for recruiting young mothers was greater than any average size home could accommodate. So I took it to the church. I was already involved in the National Women's Conference, the culmination of the visionary planning of Joyce Rogers, our pastor's wife. And it was Joyce who showed me by example the importance of the woman's influence in the home. Women need to see that there is no higher calling than to be a wife and mother.

In answer to my prayer for a ministry to meet the needs of young mothers, God was already paving the way by having in place talented workers to help. When we organized and established MOMS, it was under the able teaching of Jean Stockdale, whose husband is a staff member at Bellevue. Since that time, MOMS has grown beyond our most optimistic expectations.

It is easy to stay busy when our mindset is to work. I soon was looking at a need for a "Friend's Day," for our Women's Ministry. This is an evangelistic outreach bringing the unchurched into a circle of fellowship where they can meet new friends and acquaint themselves with the programs of the church. When a new semester of Bible Study starts in the spring and in the fall, we have a special kick-off program called, "Friends Day." It is non-denominational, and all are welcome. We have seen a tremendous increase in Bible Study over the years as a result of this ministry.

The memories of encounters with interesting people in all the places our work has taken us, are a never-ending source of pleasure to our family. Andy and Don have kept themselves available to speak of their own experiences of God's grace, and their kindness and compassion for others gives me a sense of gratitude for the men they are today. They could so easily have gone another way.

Attitude and influence work hand-in-hand, always leading upward and forward as we attempt to find the particular path assigned to us. I've no doubt that all are called to a special walkway. We all, "like sheep have gone astray," (Isa.53:6) from our chosen path, chosen from the foundation of the world. To find our way into the joy of friendship with God is a tremendous step, surprising us daily with blessing upon blessing. I do not regard attitude as optional we never have the right to choose an attitude that is harmful in any way to another. There is in each of us a siren song that calls us to the world. It's name is Pride. If the humility of Christ is lost in any prideful thought of mine, my influence for His cause is lost.

Wise, human advice is good; Christian counsel is even better, but nothing can take the place of a one on one relationship with Almighty God! He is a God of such power and compassion that before we start complaining to others, or discussing our problems with others, we need to take our honest feelings and thoughts to the only one who can actually help us. Since that morning in Bible Study in

Karen Rodgers' home, I've clung to the promise in Isaiah 65:24: *And it shall come to pass, that before they call, I will answer; and while they are yet speaking, I will hear.*

God is talking about us, *about me!* I have said in a previous chapter that this book is not offered in a "holier than thou," attitude of preaching to others, but rather, in the spirit of what I hope is humble adoration for the Savior. In speaking to others about the most important subject they will ever hear, our words are important, but I believe that the Spirit within us is even more crucial to our hearer's reception. If we are in accord with Him whose message we speak, the Lord himself will see to it that it registers in the hearts of listeners.

~ *Chapter Fifteen* ~

"We all will agree that the heartbeat of the home should originate in two hearts; the heart of the husband, and the heart of the wife, beating as one. Sadly, this isn't always the true situation. When it isn't, or when you are living alone with children to manage, what do you do? How do you solve the problem of showing outwardly what God is working within you ... each of you ... inwardly?" I was speaking to a large group of women at an Inside Out Ministry, and I had just lost my train of thought.

My sudden distraction was a young woman in a sailor dress. She was very pretty, but that was not what drew my attention to her. The audience was made up of women with high-school age daughters, but this woman looked young enough to almost *be* a teen. And she was crying as I spoke, quietly wiping away the torrent of tears that streamed down her cheeks. She seemed so troubled that I began to consciously direct my words toward her.

As soon as I was finished, she made her way to me, and asked me if she could speak to me for a few minutes. "Lisa," as I will call her here, had a very troubled marriage, as I had already guessed.

"I'll be as brief as I can," she said; "My marriage has fallen apart. My husband's attitude toward the children and me has changed so radically that I'm not sure if I can continue to stay with him."

"Changed in what way?" I asked.

"He takes no interest at all in us, he seems completely turned off to anything connected to the Lord, and he yells at the children and at me if the slightest thing goes wrong, I don't know what to do anymore, I don't feel that I can continue like this."

I immediately identified with her indecision. I could see her desperation. Not wanting to end her marriage, but not willing to continue in its present state. How well I knew the feeling!

As I spoke consolingly to Lisa, I felt such an urgency to help her. When she asked pointblank, *"What would you do?"* I answered with a question. "Does he threaten you? Are you afraid he will harm you, or the children?" After she answered negatively, I then gave her the only answer I could.

"Stick with the commitment you made to him and to God. Be smart about this! Forget about trying to change him. That's God's business. Start with you! Try to see him as you once looked at him. And don't, if it feels like it's going to *kill* you, don't complain or nag!"

Before I let her go, I gave her this final word. "Lisa, you're God's representative in this crisis. You can't be your husband's Holy Spirit. Leave that to your Lord, and concentrate on *you*; ask God to help you to be all He wants you to be, and release your husband's attitude to God!" I assured her that I would be supporting her with my prayers. I also asked her to stay in touch with me.

Since that troubled time in her life, Lisa has told me how grateful she is that God brought her to the "Inside Out" meeting that night. She had not known when we met, but God already had a very special gift in His plan for her. She was pregnant. This, of itself, seemed a miracle because after her last child was born, her doctor had performed a tubal ligation. In amazement, the doctor also informed her that the ligation was still intact.

As she began to study and seek the Holy Spirit's guidance, Lisa's attitude changed. Her genuine concern for her husband had the effect of softening his attitude. By this time, she was praying that God would give them another chance to make their home what she now believed it could be. In early spring of 1998, a beautiful, healthy baby arrived to share the happy Christian home they were building together on faith. Nothing seems to please God more than restoring relationships.

Soon after John's life changed, we had begun inviting young people into our home. We wanted Andy and Don to grow up to be the kind of adults that understand the problems facing the youth of today. Through the years, both John and I have encouraged them to invite their friends into our home.

In college, their suite mate in the athletic dorm stood six feet, five, in his sock feet. He weighed two hundred, ninety-five pounds, and was every coach's dream of a football player. Jack Oliver was a decent, kind young man, but he was not a Christian. Andy and Don invited him to a Bible Study they were attending, but he was not interested. They refused to give up on him. Andy tried to persuade him by drawing him into discussion, then preaching to him. Easy-going Don, in his low-key approach to people, just loved him.

They brought Jack home to meet us one weekend, and in those two days he found his home away from home. He was so like a family member, we fixed up a bedroom for him, using an old youth bed from storage. His feet hung off the bed a foot or more, but he didn't seem to mind. We all loved him and he gratefully soaked it up. In no time at all, he was fitting himself into Bible discussion, and he began studying it with Andy and Don. The power of the Holy Spirit working through the boys soon had Jack convicted and committed. Once converted, Jack wasted no time in seeking God's will for his own niche of service.

When his football skills attracted the attention of the pros, Jack's response was, "No, thanks. I have a higher calling." Jack was called into ministry, and enrolled and graduated from Mid-America Baptist Theological Seminary in Memphis. He now serves in Family Ministry on the staff at Idlewild Baptist Church in Tampa, Florida under Dr. Ken Whitten, a great man of God, that I also consider one of my own.

Jack is married to precious Julie, and they have three children. This big, warm, gentle giant of a man, is helping families come to the Lord and grow. What a rewarding place to serve. Just the thought of him brings a smile to my face.

~ *Chapter Sixteen* ~

I'm convinced that lives here are touched by others in ways affecting eternity far more often than we know. Someone tells a story, or an incident, and we are moved to explore its meaning. Or the anvil is struck by a hammer, and a spark flies into the atmosphere to seed the unknown. Such is the nature of a testimony of faith on the soul of a listener.

The homes from which children come forth to join the mainstream of society are crucial to the future in more ways than we realize. I shudder to think what could have happened to my sons without the early blessing of my dad's influence. He was there in their early, formative years. The hurtful result of careless irresponsibility by a family member can often be reversed by love and wise counsel. My own experience has taught me the value of always showing love to our youths as they try to cope with life's uncertainties. The "bad" boys and girls of our society are worth saving. There is no gift we can give them that was not first given to us.

I realize more fully each day the joy of involvement in the lives of young children. Both Andy and Don are now married, with children of their own. John and I, (Poppy and Nana to our grandchildren) are so blessed to have Rebecca and Rachel, (Don and Cheryl's daughters) and Hunter and Jordan (Andy and Stacy's sons) near enough to share in their interests. Thankfully, their interests at this point haven't been a cause for concern, although at five, when Rebecca was moved from one Sunday School class to another, she did seriously consider joining a different church.

"I don't want to be a Baptist anymore," she said; "I want to be one of God's chosen people. I'll be a Jew."

When I told her she couldn't be Jewish, she said, "Okay, then I'll be a Latter Day Jesus people." I also nixed that.

"Why not, Nana?" she asked. For lack of a better reason, I answered, "Because Poppy won't let you!" Satisfied with that, she said no more about it.

If, as the Bible and Life indicate, this earthly time is for learning and growing, then we are but a prep school of scholars wending our way to eternity. In the here and now, we are preparing for our final destination. God's call, and surely we know it comes to all, once spoken, places the burden of decision squarely upon us.

Unanswered, it can come again in a moment — or an eon. If we recognize its source, we are compelled to respond. Who knows if it will hang imperceptibly suspended, to await a leisurely answer? We often ignore the Lord's knock on our heart's door because we are fearful of what He will ask of us. Our fear of the unknown is not unlike a child's fear of the dentist's chair. He is told that if he will trust himself to the dentist's hands, all will come out well. Does that unseat his fear? Of course not. Jesus must have understood man's inordinate fear of all unknown possibilities because he was constantly saying to his followers, "Fear not Fear not!"

The word, fear, is often recorded in the Bible's message. There is a valid reason for it; it is one of man's most basic instincts. We have every cause to fear God's wrath. There is no book in the Bible that fails to tell or imply the omnipotence of God and His expectation of our response to Him. Scripture teaches that reverential fear of God is truly the beginning of wisdom. Aware of the difficulties we have in determining the difference between God's loving purposes and His judgments, Jesus offers us the way out of Fear's darkness and into His light. How often we see in God's Word the assuring message: *I am with thee. If God be for us, who can be against us?*

We sometimes get the idea that we understand all the underlying reasons behind what happens in life. At best, we can realize that God allows what happens, and is quite aware of the outcome. In our own reasoning, just when we get everything all figured out, we get the props knocked out from under us. That is because we stake our claim on properties and on people, and because of our human, capricious nature, our perspective is often nebulous.

We can thank the Lord that there is a way to know His purpose for us, and He will help us find it. Why aren't more people looking? Is it because they are afraid?

In the long ago past, prophets of God thundered forth their dire warnings, but few listened. And if we could compare the people of yesteryear to ourselves, we would probably find that the ratio of obedient believers in God is much the same. Why are we so reluctant to let go of our fears, and just trust our Heavenly Father?

From the day Adam and Eve tried to hide from God in the garden of Eden, people have spent their lives hunting a place where God can't find them. There is no such place.

If I take tomorrow's wings
And ascend to touch the mist of heaven's floor,
I will feel Your guiding presence,
And see Your light beside the open door!
If I spread the wings of freedom,
And descend beneath the waters of the sea…
The darkness cannot cover, for it and light
Are both alike to Thee!

This thought, lifted from the l39th Psalm, is to me both awe-inspiring and reassuring.

In rebellion against God, man is constantly running, constantly denying, always hoping to defer God's judgment. The guilty fear of God's wrath is always there, whether or not consciously acknowledged. The person does not exist who could reasonably prefer hell over heaven, but multitudes choose to hold their decision in reserve to be activated at a later date. As common intellect will tell us, time here in this life is not of our choosing.

That clarion call, *It is finished*, belongs only to our Creator. Like the painting of an artist whose brush moves simultaneously over the entire canvas to achieve a finished work, God has the option of saying when we are a finished portrayal. As only the artist knows when his masterpiece is complete, only God can say when a life here shall end. That thought is our peace and our joy when we are living in agreement with His will.

Great minds have tried and tried, in thousands of words, to convey what heaven is like. If you love God, if you can worship Him in Spirit and in truth, if you are well-versed in His word, you know as much about heaven as any person on this earth today. I accept the Apostle Paul's inspired statement that "Eye hath not seen, nor ear heard, neither have entered into the heart of man, the things which God hath prepared for them that love him." We have in Scripture many indications of what to expect of heaven, but they come to us in symbols, to be interpreted at the the Holy Spirit's discretion.

Jeremiah, the faithful, godly prophet who vehemently preached God's call to repentance, though rich in grace, had little effect on the stubborn, stiff-necked people of his day. God's message through him has been an effective warning to me many times. Jer.17:10 graphically states:

"I the Lord search the heart, I try the reins, even to give every man according to his ways, and according to the fruit of his doings."

I pose this question: If I can expect to receive in heaven according to my ways here, what will I receive there? The more troublesome question is the latter part of Jeremiah's statement: *"according to the fruit of his doings."* If I am responsible for what my ways have caused, what have my sins ultimately produced?

These questions are best answered in the light of God's inscrutable ways of righteous judgment. This is why we must openly and truthfully confess our sins to Him and trust His grace to cleanse us. A repentant, surrendered spirit always receives the blessing of His forgiveness. This was King David's secret. The secret that gave him the identifying mark, "a man after God's own heart."

When God created woman, He planted in her the instinct that is her identifying characteristic: the need to nurture. Women are called to be care-givers. There is no gift or talent more urgently needed for our present time. This gift takes various forms in its ways of ministering, but all are equally important.

My eyes were opened to our propensity to teach without realizing it is happening. My granddaughter, Rachel, at eight years old, was listening to my conversations more closely than I knew. Friends and I had discussed various scriptures concerning the end time, including the Rapture of the saints at the second coming of Christ.

Weeks later, Rachel asked me how I planned to go to heaven. Not exactly sure what she meant, I questioned her. "I know you're going," she assured me; "But I've been thinking about it, and *I've* decided to do the group thing."

"What do you mean?" I asked, with no idea what she was talking about.

"You know, Nana, the group thing, where the Christians who are alive will be caught up in the air to meet Jesus. You remember!"

Yes, I remembered, but I had thought little more about the details of the conversation. Amused, I was reminded of how quickly children learn from us when we aren't "teaching." What a joy these children's children are to us all and what a responsibility is ours as we share with them our best intents and purposes. In today's changing world, many grandparents are rearing a second set of children: their grandchildren. Older now, they find the rigors of parenthood more difficult, but their faithfulness urges them forward. They need our prayers, and in many cases, our help.

~ *Chapter Seventeen* ~

The heart of the king of Syria was sore troubled, and he called his servants and said unto them, "Will ye not show me which of us is for the king of Israel?" And one of his servants said, "None, my lord, O king: but Elisha, the prophet that is in Israel, telleth the king of Israel the words which thou speakest in thy bedchamber."

Therefore, the king of Syria sent a great force to seize the prophet, Elisha. Their number compassed the city about with horses and chariots and a great host. And the servant of the man of God was risen early and saw the surrounding army.

And he said, "Alas, my master, what shall we do?"

And Elisha said, "Fear not; for they that be with us are more than they that be with them."

And Elisha prayed, and said, "Lord, I pray thee, open his eyes, that he may see." And the Lord opened the eyes of the young man, and he saw: and behold, the mountain was full of horses and chariots of fire round about Elisha.

And when the force of Syria came down to him, Elisha prayed unto the Lord, and said, "Smite this people, I pray thee, with blindness. And he smote them with blindness, according to the word of Elisha. And Elisha led them to Samaria, and said, "Lord, open their eyes that they might see." And the Lord opened their eyes.

And Elisha prepared great provision for them; and when they had eaten and drunk, he sent them away, and they went to their master. So the bands of Syria came no more into the land of Israel. (From the sixth chapter of II Kings)

I look back on the early years of my marriage in amazement. I marvel at the undergirding strength of will that
held me in its grip in those abusive times when a part of me
wanted to give up. That strength refused to let me quit.

I am grateful that even before I knew Jesus in the inti-
macy that saved me, He knew me. He is only a heartbeat
away from us all. He hears our smallest cry.

As I continue to speak to women there is a growing
hunger in me to minister to those who are hurting to help
those who are there for answers. They want to know what
they can do to change those dreadful, unbearable times that
explode with such frequency. If any word from me could
change the suffering I see reflected in the eyes of my
spiritual sisters, I would gladly speak it.

I have been asked why I do not go into more detail about
my own humiliation and hurt. Unless it would benefit
others, I see no reason to dredge up painful memories. We
all have different personalities, as do our husbands, and we
are all motivated from our different fields of experience.
God always works individually within the heart, dealing
with the situation that is unique to each. Not all will thrive
in the same soil. The advice I shared with Lisa in another
chapter, is the only course of action I know that changes
anyone. First giving ourselves up to God, then trusting His
will for us all. I always want to state clearly that I did not
change John. After God changed me, *He* changed John in
His own way and in His own time.

There is another deeply rooted reason why the more
painful incidents are best left unsaid. John no longer
bears any resemblance to the man who seemed to take
such satisfaction from cruelty and mayhem. This man
who was, and is my husband has been the love of my life
since the day I met him. In our first meeting, I sensed that
this would be no ordinary relationship. Before I even

knew him well, I knew I would willingly give up every
future hope I had, to help him achieve his dream. Did
I make a mistake in falling so deeply in love, on sight?
There is one answer to that. It is only because of God's
grace that this story could have a happy ending.

The telling of this story of a marriage, flawed from the
beginning, is an attempt to offer an alternative to the careless breaking of sacred vows at the first sign of trouble.
Jesus warned that in this world we would have trouble.
*"These things I have spoken unto you, that in me ye might have
peace. In the world ye shall have tribulation: but be of good cheer;
I have overcome the world."* (John 16:13) His peace in us
changes everything. He is always the answer.

In deepest gratitude for what God has done in my life,
I feel compelled to make one last attempt to bring hope to
those who feel entrapped in a hopeless situation. There
ought to be a magic formula we could give to all those whose
hearts are heavy. There is none. But there is this: There is a
promise. If you haven't found yours, you must search it out
and claim it. God's Word is full of promise. In those first
days after Jesus saved me, I searched through my Bible for
something to claim for myself. One day, these words
jumped off the page and into my heart: *Behold, the Lord's
hand is not shortened, that it cannot save; neither his ear heavy,
that it cannot hear. (Isa. 59:1)* Comforting words, but loaded
with an implied condition.

I spent several days working my way through this verse
before getting the courage to accept the words that
followed. When I could see that my own attitude of
resentment was the immediate problem, I knew I was on
the right track. We must forgive. It is never easy. When we
learn to pray in spirit, and in truth, we will see results.
Earthly troubles are often God's corrective discipline.
Blessings in disguise. They are our chariots of fire that take

us to higher ground. We don't see them that way. When we are hurt, we only see defeat, not the chariot taking us into God's will.

Search your Bible for your own promises from God's hand. Look for His touch on your life each day. *It is there!*

Every great love story should have a happy ending. How blest older couples must feel to have those golden years together! How wonderful to be able to share the good memories! If it happens that John and I are allowed to walk into the sunset together, I want us to share with others the joy we've known of friendship, spiritual companionship, and always the blessed rewards of romantic love for each other. Whatever God chooses for us, whatever best serves His will, if one of us is left to walk alone, we are agreed to continue on in the joy of our Lord. The joy of the Lord is indeed, our strength.

It is my prayer that my story will resonate in the hearts of women, who like myself once hesitated to establish a viable identity. The invisible bond uniting us all was designed by a loving Heavenly Father to stretch all the way to heaven. When Jesus said we must love one another, He placed within us His enabling power to obey: the gift of the Holy Spirit. It is only when we overcome our fears and work for the good of all that we will see change. We all have gifts to offer. God placed within every woman a creative spirit with which to serve. May we unite in doing it with joy!

Behold, God is my salvation; I will trust, and not be afraid: for the Lord Jehovah is my strength and my song; He also is become my salvation.

Isaiah 12: 2

About the Authors

Nancy Bramlett continues to share her personal testimony and message at churches, conferences and to women everywhere. She loves her church, Bellevue Baptist, and has been active in the Women's Ministry for many years.

She enjoys her work with the Women's Salvation Army Auxillary in Memphis and serves as Chaplain on the Board.

She spends most of her time with John in his ministry and with their four grandchildren — Rebecca, Rachel, Hunter, and Jordan.

Tula Jeffries is a gifted writer that wrote a weekly inspirational column for the *Daily News* of Richmond, Missouri for many years.

She is the author of "Singleness of Purpose" and "Taming the Bull." She now makes her home in Nashville, Arkansas and is active in her church there.

Touched by Grace

Dearly beloved sweet sister in Christ,
What an added dimension you have brought to my life.
The gift of your friendship, presence and prayers
Encourage the weary in times of despair.
Reminiscent of Jesus faithful, gracious and kind,
A vessel of honor sanctified and refined
A portrait of beauty, the fragrance of Christ,
Fills and exudes from your exemplary life.
You bear in your body the marks of the one
Who poured out His life for the victory He won.
Having come through the fire of affliction and strife
You have the anointing of God on your life.
Though bruised in heart and forever changed
Sweet Jesus perpetually imprints His Name
In the radiant smile and life you impart
For the multiplied graces of Christ fill your heart.
Conformed to His image with joy beyond measure,
You're abandoned to God for His glory and pleasure.
Touched by grace is your countenance fair,
Highly useful to God by the witness you bear.
A far better place this old world has become
Since graced by your presence unequalled to none.

Fran A. McDaniel
'97

Then those who feared the Lord spoke to one another;
And the Lord listened and heard them;
So a book of remembrance was written for those who fear
The Lord, and who meditate on His name.
Malachi 3:16